Keeping Your Adoptive Family Strong

of related interest

Attaching Through Love, Hugs and Play
Simple Strategies to Help Build Connections with Your Child
Deborah D. Gray
ISBN 978 1 84905 939 8
eISBN 978 0 85700 753 7

Let's Learn About Adoption
The Adoption Club Therapeutic Workbook on
Adoption and Its Many Different Forms
Regina M. Kupecky
ISBN 978 1 84905 762 2
eISBN 978 0 85700 997 5
Part of the Adoption Club series

Welcoming a New Brother or Sister Through Adoption
Arleta James
ISBN 978 1 84905 903 9
eISBN 978 0 85700 653 0

Love and Mayhem
One Big Family's Uplifting Story of Fostering and Adoption
John DeGarmo
ISBN 978 1 84905 775 2
eISBN 978 1 78450 012 2

The Unofficial Guide to Adoptive Parenting
The Small Stuff, The Big Stuff and The Stuff In Between
Sally Donovan
Foreword by Dr. Vivien Norris
Foreword by Jim Clifford OBE and Sue Clifford
ISBN 978 1 84905 536 9
eISBN 978 0 85700 959 3

Why Can't My Child Behave?
Empathic Parenting Strategies that Work
for Adoptive and Foster Families
Amber Elliott
ISBN 978 1 84905 339 6
eISBN 978 0 85700 671 4

Preparing for Adoption
Everything Adopting Parents Need to Know About
Preparations, Introductions and the First Few Weeks
Julia Davis
Foreword by Hugh Thornbery
ISBN 978 1 84905 456 0
eISBN 978 0 85700 831 2

"With *Keeping Your Adoptive Family Strong*, Keck and Gianforte deliver a timely and incredibly helpful resource for those beginning the journey of adoption and professionals working in the field. The book gives an honest look at what to expect when adopting from foster care, and it is armed with realistic—rather than romanticized—expectations that give parents the keys to successfully overcome the inherent challenges. Consistent with our organization's experiences working within the largest foster care system in the US, *Keeping Your Adoptive Family Strong* shows that adoption won't be easy, but is a journey well worth taking for anyone with room in their heart to change the course of a child's life."

—*Janis Spire, President and CEO, Alliance*
for Children's Rights, Los Angeles

"*Keeping Your Adoptive Family Strong* combines all the essential elements that make up an important book—knowledge, insight, experience, honesty, and heart—into one very accessible and readable volume. I believe it will genuinely help a lot of people, and I wholeheartedly recommend it to professionals and families alike."

—*Adam Pertman, President of the National Center on Adoption*
and Permanency and author of Adoption Nation

"*Keeping Your Adoptive Family Strong* is a valuable tool for prospective adoptive parents. Traumatized children often bring with them more than anyone can see. This book brings all possibilities to the forefront. It is a true and real account of what adoptive families may endure as they adjust to creating and becoming a family. Having adopted three children, two of whom experienced trauma in their young lives, my husband and I consider this book a godsend. Adoption is an incredible journey, and resources such as this will benefit not just parents, but adoptive children as well, helping them to understand where they came from and what they bring to their new families."

—*Missy Hokanson, adoptive mother*

"Although adoption offers the hope of a 'forever family', naïve good intentions and wishes for happy ever after can leave families alone in—and blamed for—their predictable crises. The authors provide a balanced approach that honestly explores the challenges and risks—while still offering reassurance and hope—by highlighting strategies that can help resolve traumatic reactions and forge resilient connections. This book should be a must read for anyone involved in adoption, whether as a parent or professional."

—Vicky Kelly PsyD, MSW, MHA Director,
Delaware Division of Family Services

"Keck and Gianforte speak directly, with great honesty, empathy, wisdom and humor, to those most closely involved in adoption: adopters themselves and their professional supporters. They attempt to unpick the myths, misconceptions, and misplaced attributions of blame surrounding the placement and support of children and adolescents in adoptive families. Their practical, user-friendly, no-nonsense approach goes right to the heart of what it means, and how it feels to be, or to live with, a traumatized child. There are challenging lessons for all of us which the warmth, love, and hard-hitting humor of the authors allows us to 'hear' and accept—to set in motion the systemic and personal changes needed for adopted youngsters to rebuild their lives and thrive."

—Caroline Archer, adoptive parent, therapeutic parent mentor
and co-author of Reparenting the Child who Hurts

c.1

Keeping Your Adoptive Family Strong

Strategies for Success

GREGORY C. KECK AND L. GIANFORTE

FOREWORD BY RITA L. SORONEN

Jessica Kingsley *Publishers*
London and Philadelphia

First published in 2015
by Jessica Kingsley Publishers
73 Collier Street
London N1 9BE, UK
and
400 Market Street, Suite 400
Philadelphia, PA 19106, USA

www.jkp.com

Library of Congress Cataloging in Publication Data
A CIP catalog is available from the Library of Congress

British Library Cataloguing in Publication Data
A CIP catalogue record for this book is available from the British Library

ISBN 978 1 84905 784 4
eISBN 978 1 78450 028 3

Printed and bound in the United States

To my grandson, Jackson—you are the cutest and happiest little boy I know, and you are lucky to have parents who love you so much.
GCK

To my mother, my very first best friend.
LG

Contents

Foreword

RITA L. SORONEN

President and CEO, Dave Thomas Foundation for Adoption

In "Four Quartets," a mysteriously beautiful poem by T.S. Eliot, he notes, "Home is where one starts from. As we grow older the world becomes stranger, the pattern more complicated." For decades, scholars and weekend readers alike have dissected every phrase in the poem for meaning. To me, at many levels, the verse reflects the particularly complex landscape too many of our children experience as they make the arduous journey from abusive or neglectful homes to the confusion of foster care and finally into the strange and life-changing world of an adoptive family.

Yet their difficult trek does not end, but only just begins again, at adoption. Children and youth who have suffered trauma at the hands of the very adults who were supposed to keep them safe, who have moved multiple times while in foster care, who may have been separated from their siblings, who were re-abused while in care or who simply have not had ongoing support to address their very real nightmares, fears, and needs—cannot make the leap to adoption with ease. Nor should they. Survival is the lens through which a traumatized child views the adults and systems that surround him. Parents must be prepared to recognize, respect, and respond appropriately to a child's deep issues of loss, grief, anger, fear, and anxiety.

Last year, more than 50,000 children were adopted from foster care in the United States. While there should always be a sense of urgency in ensuring that each of the more than 100,000 children still waiting to be adopted will be placed with safe and nurturing families, there must be an equally pressing drive to equip adoptive parents with all of the tools and resources available to help them understand the child to whom they have made a lifetime commitment.

Love is required, but it is simply not enough for the adopted child. Patience is essential, but it will be tested. Informed understanding is critical, but some days, nothing will make sense. In *Keeping Your Adoptive Family Strong*—and as an important companion to his previous groundbreaking works, *Adopting the Hurt Child*, *Parenting the Hurt Child*, and *Parenting Adopted Adolescents*—Dr. Gregory Keck and his co-author Elle Gianforte skillfully weave the thoughts of parents, children, and adult adoptees with real family stories and experiences.

All parents who adopt must read this book. In fact, any individual who connects with a child while he is in foster care or after he has been adopted—from teachers and therapists to caseworkers and extended family members—will be better prepared to serve as that child's advocate and supporter with this book in hand.

Again quoting T.S. Eliot, "Every moment of our lives marks a beginning and an end." For adopted children and their parents, every moment together as a family is an opportunity to understand and honestly address the burdens of a traumatic past while working toward a strong family and future where the child can be at the center of healing, hope, and celebration.

Acknowledgments

Greg

It shouldn't be necessary to have to think so long about the people I want to thank—but I did. I come first to my sons, Brian and James, whose life experiences before adoption forever affected my life. They brought with them so much—some of it great and some of it not so great. There were times when I thought, *I have had to do so much more for them than my parents did for me.* And soon thereafter I would think, *That's not true. My parents gave me the very foundation of life in my earliest years, and that provided me with the opportunities to become who I have become.* So while I may have done more things for my sons as young adults than my parents did for me, that's simply what I felt that I needed and wanted to do. The opportunity to parent two adolescents into adulthood allowed me to live what I do professionally and what I have written about, and it gave me insights that I am able to use in my work. Brian and James, I am so glad that you have followed your dreams and are doing things that you enjoy—Brian, developing a business and career in the wrestling/mixed martial arts (MMA)/Ultimate Fighting Championship (UFC) field; James, being a co-owner of a semi-professional football team and being such a great dad to Jackson.

Of course, once again, I thank my parents, grandparents, and sister for support throughout my life. The loss of my mother two years ago has heightened my awareness about the intense feelings associated with loss. During her funeral, as I sat with my sons who lost their mothers years ago, I thought about their losses at such young ages and just how profound loss is.

Finally, I warmly thank Elle Gianforte for her partnership through the three previous books she edited and for agreeing to co-author *Keeping Your Adoptive Family Strong*. Her insights as an adoptive mother certainly strengthen her grasp of the topic, and her well-honed writing and editing skills allow our message to be delivered with a clear and powerful voice.

Elle

I must begin with a big shout-out to my son Marco, who came up with the idea to end the book with stories from adult adoptees. I just love it when you dazzle me, kiddo.

I send a huge hug across the miles to my son Ty, who grew up to be more like me than I ever thought possible. We're stuck with each other—for better or for worse—and I couldn't be happier about that.

A great deal of inspiration comes from Jenna and Aiden, who prove every day that the cycle of abuse and neglect can end. Jenna, you are a superb mother, and I love you both very much.

As always, I am enormously grateful to my husband, Joseph, who is everything I have ever wanted in a partner. You are the most loving and encouraging man I know, and I am blessed that you chose me.

I thank my parents, who taught me about the importance of family. You're with me every minute of every day, and I will carry you in my heart forever.

I extend masses of love to all my Pennella and Gianforte cousins. You have been like siblings throughout my life, and you continue to make the journey a joyful one.

Saving the best for last, I thank my co-author, Greg Keck, for including me in this project. You are so talented and knowledgeable, and working with you is always a fabulous ride. I truly believe we're the best team ever!

Both authors

Together, we thank Jessica Kingsley Publishers for encouraging us to write this book. Stephen Jones has been a joy to work with, and he probably qualifies as one of the most responsive people on the planet. Danielle McLean and Emma Holak helped pull all the components together, and their roles were vital ones that kept the project on track and made us feel well cared for.

Rita Soronen, president and CEO of the Dave Thomas Foundation for Adoption, has honored us with an insightful foreword that both touches the heart and stimulates the mind, and our gratitude and appreciation for her support of this book is boundless.

Thanks to photographer Matt Johnson and the Hutcherson family for the beautiful cover photo. It completely captures the essence of the happy adoptive family!

We are enormously grateful to our beta readers—Jan Fishler, Merille Glover, and Anne-Marie Fleckenstein—for their fresh perspective and valuable feedback.

We also extend heartfelt thanks to our old friends, new friends, and friends of friends who so openly shared the stories of their adoptions. This book wouldn't exist without you.

Disclaimer

Some of the anecdotal illustrations in this book are true to life and are included with the permission of the persons involved. All other illustrations are composites of real situations, and any resemblance to people living or dead is coincidental.

In the absence of a gender-neutral singular pronoun, the authors use the male form throughout the book for ease of readability.

In spite of the serious subject matter, you'll find a bit of humor in this book. It is the authors' sincerest hope that readers will not be offended, because in the light of difficult situations, a well-placed chuckle—or even just a smile—can work wonders to alleviate stress.

Preface

Welcoming a new child into the home through adoption is a life-changing experience—for the child, the parents, and everyone else in the family. Fantasies constantly bump into realities, sending emotions spinning in multiple directions as parents and siblings try to adjust to the change. Perhaps the only person who is truly in touch with the situation is the adopted child, who is pretty sure that living with a bunch of strangers is not going to be fun.

If the child has experienced trauma prior to adoption, the complexities of the situation multiply. While parents often see themselves as the poor victim's savior, the child usually sees a major disruption that adds to the earlier trauma. The family of origin disappears, replaced by new faces, new demeanors, new environments, and new experiences.

It's like being born in Siberia and moving to Miami. The weather may be more pleasant, it might feel really good to ditch the hat with the earflaps, but it's still a very different place. Is it better? Yes, in many respects. But the fact that it's not the norm is where the problem lies. Adapting becomes a task in itself, and it's not an easy one to master. The bottom line is this: when parents and children approach adoption from opposite directions—when one sees salvation where the other sees disconnection—the already challenging journey becomes fraught with unnecessary twists and turns.

It is a sad fact that an extreme level of denial permeates the adoption world. Social workers do not always tell parents about the challenges they might face, and many mothers and fathers do not want to hear it anyway. In their quest to create a family, they have a romanticized concept of what it will be like. With hearts full of love and heads full of dreams, they refuse to look at the real picture. Unwittingly, they are undermining their efforts and compromising their successes, because acknowledging the facts—no matter how difficult or painful—is the first step toward building a strong family.

Cynthia, adoptive mom of six-year-old Tess, was thrown into a tailspin when her first parent–teacher conference painted her daughter as an extremely aggressive and disruptive first-grader. Because the child was relatively well behaved at home, Cynthia convinced herself that the teacher simply didn't like Tess. Her response to the situation was to move her daughter to another school, and another, and another. She just couldn't believe that so many teachers really, really hated her kid!

Suzanne was concerned about her adopted son's antisocial behavior. At nine years old, Cyrus was manipulative and controlling—of his friends, his parents, his siblings, even the family dog. After reading about reactive attachment disorder, a condition that occurs when an infant fails to attach securely to a primary caregiver, Suzanne attended a weekend conference on the subject. After listening intently to every speaker, she returned home and reported to her husband, "I'm so glad I went! Cyrus is nothing like those kids I heard about!"

The actual facts: Both Tess and Cyrus were ultimately diagnosed with attachment issues. Tess was able to mask her anger at home, but her aggression surfaced when she was around her classmates. Since her mother didn't see the negative behaviors, she chose to believe they didn't exist. From a coping perspective, it was far easier for her to pin the problem on the child's teachers.

Cyrus was a textbook case, exhibiting multiple symptoms of attachment disorder that his mother refused to see—even when they were spelled out for her by experts in the field. Although the wake-up calls were late in coming, both mothers eventually acknowledged the truth and took the necessary steps to get their children into appropriate therapy.

Taking a look at the flip side

Whatever the motive for adopting—to create a family, to rescue a child, to respond to a spiritual calling—parents must face the fact that most of the children available for adoption today have sustained some sort of trauma. From physical abuse to emotional abuse, from sexualization to neglect, something dreadful has happened to place these children in the system.

What is visible: Kelsey, age ten, has red curls that form a tousled halo around her head. Her eyes are an intense blue, and she's skilled at pushing out her bottom lip to create the most heartbreaking pout. *What can't be seen:* Her father and older brother have been sexually abusing her since she was five years old.

What is visible: Malcolm, age seven, loves to play soccer. He is a natural athlete, and his skill on the field is impressive. *What can't be seen:* He and his two brothers have lived in squalor all of their young lives, sharing a single bed in a vermin-infested apartment completely under the radar of social services.

What is visible: Daniela and Dante, three-year-old twins, have the same dark eyes, husky laugh, and love of mint-chip ice cream. *What can't be seen:* Turned over at birth to the care of their grandparents because of a drug-addicted mother, their most basic needs have been systematically ignored and neglected. Says their grandmother, "It's not my fault! Twins are a lot of work!"

These are the children in need of permanent homes, a secure and stable environment, and the promise of nurturing parents, but the solution isn't quite that straightforward. Because their trauma has become an integrated part of who they are, they do not leave their hurtful experiences behind. Instead, they carry them forward into the new family, imposing their stress on the very people who are trying to end it.

Adoptive parents must keep in mind that they are taking on the complete package—not just the innocent child who needs a loving family. They must learn to immunize themselves against the potential disturbances that are moving into their home: emotional and behavioral dysregulation, sexualized behaviors, developmental immaturity, poor cause-and-effect thinking, and lack of conscience. They must avoid tumbling into the false belief that love and stability will make everything fine, because it's going to take more than that. A lot more.

A good place to start on the road to reality is to view the situation from the child's perspective. Abuse is what he has come to perceive as the norm, and he believes that his experiences are the same as everyone else's. A young child does not have the cognitive ability to realize that not everyone lives in a chaotic household, has to fend for food, or is regularly locked away. Parents who scream at each other, who inject drugs into their veins, who disappear for days at a time, who hit their little ones—this is the life the child knows. He is not aware that on the other side of town, children are laughing with their parents, sitting down together to a nutritious meal, getting cozy in their beds while Mom or Dad reads a story. He doesn't fantasize about these things and he doesn't wish for these things, because he doesn't know they exist.

When a child's idea of love is abuse, he will do everything in his power to try to get his adoptive parents to mistreat him. It's what he knows and has come to expect. It's familiar. And in some bizarre way, it's comfortable. Of course, this doesn't mean he will succeed, but it does mean he'll push buttons and test limits in ways that unprepared parents cannot even begin to imagine.

Louisa and Marc adopted four-year-old Patrick shortly after moving into a new home. Blonde and green eyed, Patrick was a handsome child with a solemn expression and a controlled façade. Late one spring afternoon, in anticipation of dinner guests, Louisa was busy in the kitchen preparing her famous vegetable lasagna. Patrick was playing outside with a neighborhood child, and she could hear their voices rising and falling through the open window.

When she walked into the dining room to set the table a few minutes later, she was surprised to see Patrick standing there. She hadn't heard him enter the house, and his playmate was nowhere to be seen. What was visible, however, was a set of muddy footprints than extended the length of the dining room and ended at the child's feet.

"Patrick, what have you done?" Louisa exclaimed. Her head was a jumble of thoughts: *new house, new carpeting, big bucks, bad kid.*

"I didn't do it," Patrick answered calmly.

"But you're standing at the end of a line of muddy footprints!" Louisa said, sure that logic would win out.

"Not mine," he replied in the same maddeningly cool tone.

Her voice rising, Louisa tried reasoning with him again. "But, Patrick, they must be yours! You and I are the only people in the house, and you're the one who's been playing outside. If you'll just admit it, I promise I won't punish you."

"I don't know what you're talking about. I already told you—they're not mine." With that, he sauntered into the kitchen—leaving another wave of footprints behind him—and poured himself a glass of milk.

Angry with her son for muddying up the room (*Guests would be arriving in a few hours!*), upset that he'd lied to her, and furious that he was so cavalier about it, Louisa grabbed him by the arm, ignoring the milk that sloshed onto the kitchen floor. She roughly led him up the stairs and into his room, where she told him to stay until he was ready to tell the truth.

"I don't care if you're here until you're 12!" she shouted, her face growing red. "Misbehaving and then lying about it is not what we do in this family!" She slammed the door behind her, already beginning to regret her outburst. She stood in the hallway for a few minutes, recovering enough to try to reason with Patrick again. After all, she was the parent; he was the child. Surely she was the one in charge, capable of handling the situation with more grace and less noise. When she gently opened the door just a crack, she saw him sitting on the edge of his bed, a grin of pure satisfaction spread wide across his face.

Patrick, it seems, had gotten precisely what he wanted. He was shouted at, manhandled, alienated, and grounded. This new mom must really love him a lot!

Facing reality without fear

Keeping your adoptive family strong is a challenge, to be sure, but it's not an insurmountable one. It begins with pursuing the cold, hard facts, followed by a strong conviction to face the not-so-easy, didn't-see-that-coming aspects of opening the door to a child in need. Yes, there will be emotional turmoil. Yes, there will be secondary trauma experienced by other members of the family. But forewarned is forearmed, as they say. The more parents know about what to expect, the better equipped they are to rise to the challenges they will face.

While the process itself might not be easy, the keys to a healthy and functional adoptive family are quite basic.

- accessibility to honest, accurate information about the child's background

- willingness to recognize and accept things for what they are

- support, compassion, and understanding from family, friends, and mental health professionals

- the comfort that stems from knowing that other families face similar difficulties

- confidence in the ability to succeed.

The information needed for survival and success is available. It just takes the strength to look, to listen, to accept, and to act accordingly. Whatever shape the family takes—a mom and a dad, two moms, two dads, just one parent; multiple siblings or an only child—the innate desire of most adoptive parents is to make that family the best it can be. To do it correctly, they must operate from a position rooted in the reality of their individual situation. There's no pretending, defending, rationalizing, or lying. There's no faking it, ignoring it, rejecting it, or justifying it. There's only looking the truth in the eye and staring it down with the utmost conviction.

It can be done. It has been done. This book shares stories of parents and children who have weathered the storms of adoption and emerged into the sunshine. While not every tale has a happy ending, the successes are joyful, heartwarming, and encouraging.

Sometimes it means lowering the bar. Sometimes it means shifting gears in the middle of the ride. And sometimes it means running off for a quiet moment to regroup and recoup. Whatever form the journey takes, parents must keep sight of the fact that it is driven by hope and fueled by the desire to make a difference in the life of a child. With that objective in mind, the destination will always be clear.

CHAPTER 1

The Impact of Trauma on Human Development

Most contemporary adoption professionals agree that the majority of children available for adoption have experienced some sort of trauma, which is why they're in the system in the first place. Perhaps the only exceptions are those infants whose adoptions were thoughtfully planned and arranged by birth parents in concert with attorneys and/or adoption agencies—infants whose experiences *in utero* and during their earliest days were devoid of conflict and misery. We'll call them the lucky ones. The rest—representing the vast majority of today's adoptions—involve infants, children, and adolescents who were removed from their birth families by the child welfare system in their respective countries or abandoned by their parents and placed in orphanage care.

Representing a smaller group of adoptees are those children who have been institutionalized in orphanages from "sending countries" around the world, defined as places with significant numbers of children who are adopted by people outside the country. These regions—including China, Guatemala, India, Colombia, and Ethiopia—typically make children available to foreigners because very few of their own residents adopt. Several of these sending countries are now attempting to move away from orphanage care and are even encouraging in-country adoptions.

Regardless of the source—domestic or international, birth family or institution—virtually all adoptees today have endured trauma on some level.

Children who are adopted from foster care have been in the system as the result of physical abuse, sexual abuse, neglect, or serious ongoing domestic violence. They become available for adoption when it is determined that they cannot safely be reunited with their birth families. This decision is sometimes made after several years and multiple foster placements, which creates additional stress for an already traumatized child.

The result is a population of children who have been removed, returned, re-placed, and essentially recycled. With each change, the trauma builds and the child's suffering escalates. Let's take a look at the progression of the pattern.

- Trauma occurs in the birth home, often repeatedly.

- The rescue process adds new trauma as the child is removed from what is familiar.

- Multiple placements into strange new environments add more trauma.

- Returning to the birth home and losing attachments that might have been made in the foster home(s) creates still more trauma.

- Subsequent removal from the birth home generates additional trauma.

- And the cycle continues.

Sound complicated and confusing? If merely reading about it makes your head spin, imagine how complex this circuitous process is for the child. And if that isn't chaotic enough, the adoptive family is likely to experience the ripples of the child's trauma over time.

The diagnosis

For many years, the most commonly used diagnosis for individuals who have had exposure to trauma has been post-traumatic stress disorder (PTSD). Developed in the post-Vietnam War era, the PTSD diagnosis made its way into the general population rather quickly and was commonly seen in the child welfare system.

The disorder is routinely applied to children and adolescents who have been victims of neglect and abuse, and, in fact, is among the most frequently used diagnoses for children in the system.

While PTSD somewhat captures the symptoms seen in many children who have been traumatized within their families, there is another diagnosis frequently seen, but not officially recognized, by child welfare workers and mental health professionals. This diagnosis is called complex trauma, sometimes referred to as developmental trauma disorder.

In a report compiled by members of the National Child Traumatic Stress Network (NCTSN), complex trauma is defined as:

> the dual problem of children's exposure to traumatic events and the impact of this exposure on immediate and long-term outcomes. Complex traumatic exposure refers to children's experiences of multiple traumatic events that occur within the caregiving system—the social environment that is supposed to be the source of safety and stability in a child's life. Typically, complex trauma exposure refers to the simultaneous or sequential occurrences of child maltreatment—including emotional abuse and neglect, sexual abuse, physical abuse, and witnessing domestic violence—that are chronic and begin in early childhood.[1]

It is probably safe to say there is not a single child in the custody of a child protective agency who has endured just one harmful incident. Children who are living in abusive families may often experience ongoing maltreatment before coming to the attention of child welfare professionals. And very young children under the age of one or two could easily be victimized without detection, since they are often not seen by anyone outside the family who might report abuse or neglect.

When social workers do get involved, they might only be aware of the reported incident and know nothing of preceding events. In such cases, official records reflect only an isolated occurrence, when, in reality, there may have been long-term problems that significantly intensified the amount of the child's trauma.

Complex trauma, complex family system

Life can become very convoluted when an unsuspecting family adds a child or adolescent who has lived through repetitive trauma. While most families adopting from the foster system have information about the details of the child's life, they most often do not understand the depth and gravity of how those early experiences affect psychosocial and biological development. More unfortunate still, they have probably not examined how dramatically the child's trauma can affect all members of the family.

"When we decided to adopt Jeremy at the age of 14, the agency provided us with volumes of written material regarding his background," reports the boy's dad. "He had been in foster care for several years, so reams of paperwork had accumulated. There were many accounts of the abuse allegations that had occurred prior to his being permanently removed from his family. We were told that Jeremy, like most individuals with trauma histories, was developmentally immature but would probably catch up once he was placed and adopted.

"My wife and I thought we knew what immature meant, but what we had undertaken was infinitely more than that. Jeremy's so-called immaturity resulted in rages for hours at a time, constant harassment of our other children, walls with dozens of non-decorative holes in them, and beloved family pets that would run for cover whenever he entered the room. There were many days when living with Jeremy felt as if we were involved in genetic warfare instead of an adoption. Much of the time, it felt as if the entire birth family we read about had moved into our home and taken up permanent residence.

"Every aspect of Jeremy's life had been affected by his earlier experiences. I suppose we should have known that on some level, but I guess we were too naïve. What we did come to understand, though, was that our lives were not as much under our control as they had been prior to the adoption.

"Our other kids became really angry with my wife and me. One night, after a particularly bad episode on Jeremy's part, my daughter shouted, 'What were you thinking? You can't just go get someone who has lived in a crazy family, bring them here, and think they'll be normal!' It was a real wake-up call. I mean, if a 12-year-old could figure this out, what *were* we thinking?"

To their credit, this well-meaning couple were thinking that they could add another person to their family, help an adolescent who had endured a difficult life, and ultimately witness him evolve into a stable, productive person—the kind of person he could have been from the start if circumstances had been different. These are all very warm and fuzzy thoughts and expectations, but they fail to take into consideration the life-long consequences of trauma.

The parents also failed to acknowledge how the lives of every family member would change in a reverse/parallel way to Jeremy's. They became confused and disoriented when they realized they were altering in a way that was completely foreign to them. They had never before felt the almost constant anxiety about what would happen next. They were unfamiliar with the kind of emotional arousal they experienced on a nearly daily basis, and they were becoming reactive instead of proactive.

"We started out expecting Jeremy to change," adds his mom, "but instead, we were the ones who were changing. We were morphing into people we didn't recognize—people we didn't even like. We were a living reflection of Jeremy's problems: easily frustrated and easily angered. Both my husband and I felt impotent as people and incompetent as parents. Jeremy was systematically sucking the energy out of all of us, and we were changing more than he was."

While his parents knew much of what had happened to Jeremy as a young child, they hadn't given serious thought to how deeply his early abuse had hurt him and how long his emotional pain would last. Adding to the problem, they had not considered how any of this would affect their family as a whole.

Adoption preparation, although better than it once was, tends to focus on the positive aspects of family building. While this tactic makes some sense, it does nothing to prepare families for post-adoption shock and the depression that follows. If parents had some insight into just how serious and lasting many trauma-related issues are, a lot of their misery could be mitigated.

As was the case with Jeremy's parents, prospective adopters are often told that behavioral difficulties will subside once the child has a permanent home. This kind of prognostication is simply not true.

There is no hard evidence to support the belief that the presence of a new family will magically and immediately eliminate the severe damage that has occurred to the psyche and biology of a traumatized child.

Realistically, why would anyone think that simple relocation could possibly eliminate an intrinsic disorder? If you were chronically depressed and living in Ohio, would your life be any better if you moved to New Jersey? You'd still be depressed—only with nice beaches.

Healthy, then not so much

Trauma causes profound brain alterations. They require specialized intervention, such as neurofeedback, which may train and regulate the brain to its optimal functioning. Love and nurturing certainly help, but if they cannot be received by the child due to neurological impairment, they fall on infertile land.

Most adoptive families are healthy prior to the arrival of a child with a history of complex trauma, but that is likely to fade. By the time they seek out the help of mental health professionals, they often appear out of control and irrational. This unfortunate state is a response to the challenges involved in parenting a child with complex trauma issues. Many mental health professionals who are not familiar with childhood maltreatment do not understand the dynamics of what occurs when parents incorporate a traumatized child into their family.

Mai was adopted from China when she was nine. Although she made a few superficial efforts to join her new family, her early trauma kept getting in the way—seriously, life threateningly in the way.

When she was ten, Mai climbed a tree in pursuit of the family cat and threw the feline to the ground. Four months later, she attempted to kill her younger sister by holding her under water in the bathtub. The child's thrashing saved her, but fear permeated the family.

Distressed beyond belief, Mai's parents turned to their social worker for help, and the child was placed in a psychiatric facility. During her evaluation, Mai described a very elaborate plan to murder her parents. Even though it was unlikely that she could have implemented such a complex plot at the age of ten, the details were startling and horrifying. When asked to share the specifics of her scheme with her mom and dad, she did so with no reluctance and great enthusiasm. Yet in spite of her outlandish and bizarre admission, mental health professionals continued to judge and blame her parents, harshly and openly.

"You're angry," they said.

Who wouldn't be angry if someone tried to kill their child and the family pet?

"You just need to relax," they said.

How relaxed would you be in the presence of an aspiring murderer?

For years, the professionals who are supposedly well versed in such issues assessed Mai's parents inaccurately. For years, the parents' level of suffering increased as the blame for their child's behavior continued to fall on them.

When Mai was 16, she brought a kitchen knife to school and threatened her classmates with it. Amazingly, no one was hurt. But when Mai was hauled off in handcuffs by the police, the professionals finally took notice.

There is no acceptable explanation as to why the alleged experts consistently miss the obvious dynamics in families with seriously disturbed children. Their first course of intervention is usually to analyze the adoptive parents, which is ignorant, at the very least, and possibly unethical. It's one thing to blame the mom and dad if the family has several birth children, all of whom manifest major problems; in such cases, the parents just might have issues that contribute to the dysfunction of their offspring. But why would anyone with a shred of common sense attribute blame to parents who adopted a traumatized child? (If you're sensing a degree of anger and exasperation here, you're right.) When a previously traumatized child joins a healthy family at the age of nine, bringing with her a load of baggage, why on earth blame the adoptive parents? It seems so unreservedly simple minded, and it can't possibly encourage the parents to support their troubled child and facilitate corrective emotional experiences.

Blame creates defensiveness, and defensiveness leads to inaction or ineffective action. Family after family have reported that they have worked with multiple therapists who do not seem to understand the dynamics of the family. In most instances, they tend to assume that the difficulties are based on the parents' attitudes and behaviors and the family's day-to-day activities. There is often no recognition of the role that the child's early trauma plays and how it contributes to the dysfunction that is seen in families with hurt children.

Trauma may completely overwhelm a parent's ability to cope, often resulting in the consumption and depletion of fundamental life-management skills. When there is a violation of a person's familiar ideas and expectations, he is put in a state of confusion and insecurity. He experiences cognitive dissonance, which then impairs his capacity to parent at his maximum potential.

Professionals who are not cognizant of the dynamics of complex trauma may miss the critical components of what is actually occurring in the adoptive family. It becomes easy to assume that the child's behavioral issues are the result of the parents' dynamics. An unprepared therapist may then assume that the anger and frustrations expressed by the parents are the cause of the child's maladaptive behaviors. Within a family system, the transfer of the child's traumatic feelings to the parents or siblings is very common, and this point is missed by many people who are supposed to support the family, such as teachers, therapists, and religious leaders.

So try this for a change, experts: assume that the messy state of the family is a *response* to the challenges involved in parenting a child with complex trauma issues. Then see where that assumption takes you. It could be the beginning of something truly enlightening.

Laying the groundwork for adoption

Pre-adoptive expectations may not be met if the parents have not been properly prepared—and *properly* is the operative word. If the parents have not been informed of the seriousness of what could potentially happen post-placement, they will likely be blindsided by whatever the child or adolescent presents.

Expectations are extremely important, because they lay the foundation for how people enter new experiences. When these expectations are unmet—or worse still, violated—individuals feel betrayed, angry, and misled. Some of the most common expectations expressed by adoptive parents are:

- "My partner will support me."

- "Good parenting will resolve the child's past issues."

- "My faith will remain strong."

- "My extended family and my friends will be encouraging and understanding."

- "Professionals will believe me and help me with any difficulties that may arise."

- "I will be able to manage any problems I may face."

- "The child I adopt will be happy to be settled into a new family."

- "I won't have to deal with the kinds of atrocious issues that were discussed in adoption training."

- "My family life will remain the same as it was before adoption."

Sadly, for many families, these simple expectations are not realized. If there are two parents, their relationship may begin to erode. Traumatized kids often focus their anger on their new mothers, because they believe it is a mother's job to protect their children from harm. Since that did not happen in their birth families, they ascribe their anger and pain to their adoptive mothers, consequently creating more chaos for their moms than their dads. In fact, fathers may not even see the worst behaviors, which remain reserved for the mothers, until long after the mother is overwhelmed. Furthermore, her frustration may be exacerbated by the fact that her husband may not believe her claims about the new kid's intolerable attitude.

Sebastian was adopted from an orphanage in South America at the age of ten. He had experienced a great deal of abuse before being removed from his family, and his stay in the orphanage was complicated by many difficult behaviors. When he met Barbara and

Scott, his adoptive parents, he was utterly charming. The three had daily visits for almost two months, and Barbara and Scott were delighted to discover that they were having fun in their new roles.

Sebastian seemed to relate to his new parents equally well, which came as a pleasant surprise to Barbara and Scott. The hours of training they had received included a lot of information about trauma and its impact on children, but their son seemed to have lucked out. Everything appeared to be going extremely well, and they were anxious to go home with Sebastian and proudly show him off to the rest of the family.

After about two months of uneventful settling in, Barbara began to have uncomfortable feelings that she could neither understand nor explain. These emotions made her feel guilty, and she worried that something was wrong with her.

"Why can't I feel close to Sebastian?" she lamented. "What am I doing that is causing him to pull away from me? He seems to be getting closer to his dad. Maybe I'm just not cut out to be a mom."

In the meantime, Sebastian and Scott were playing ball together, going on hikes, and enjoying a developing father–son relationship. Barbara, on the other hand, was seeing a completely different side of her child. At times, he was openly defiant with her when Scott was away from home, and she finally decided to discuss her concerns and feelings of isolation with her husband. To her amazement, Scott had no idea that she was having such unsettling feelings. He even questioned her credibility, suggesting that she might be overreacting. Barbara was not happy.

As the tension in the relationship between Sebastian and Barbara grew, his acting out increased in proportion. In the mornings, after Scott left for work, Sebastian would push button after button to annoy his mom, then cheerfully jump on the school bus as if nothing had happened. Barbara became more aware of her mounting anger and frustrations, which were directed at both her child and her spouse. By this time, father and son had become best buddies. Scott, feeling a bit cocky about his success in building such a solid relationship with Sebastian, took an accusatory stance with his wife.

"If only you were more patient, he would probably feel more comfortable with you. I've never seen the problems you complain about. I guess I believe you, but I just can't imagine those behaviors."

Feeling as if she was running out of options, Barbara proposed an experiment. She asked Scott to pretend to leave for work one morning, and then keep out of sight. His exasperation evident in his exaggerated sigh, he reluctantly agreed, hiding in the pantry while Barbara prepared breakfast. As soon as Sebastian walked into the kitchen, his verbal abuse of Barbara began.

"You know I hate scrambled eggs!' he bellowed. "How can you be so stupid? I swear, if you put them in front of me, I'm going to throw the plate in your face!"

Surprise, Scott—you're not the better parent, after all. You're simply not your son's chosen victim.

Isolation

Families unfamiliar with living with trauma are unnerved by their new experiences. They often feel isolated, because they are judged or disbelieved by family and friends when they try to share pieces of the strange new world they live in. They go to their places of worship, only to hear how beautiful their adopted daughter is. They can barely resist telling people about the hell they had to go through just to get her to dress and get in the car that morning. The more that people fawn over her, the less comfortable they feel about sharing anything. As time goes on, many families abandon their churches, temples, and mosques and minimize visits with extended family members. They often do not even get to spend quiet time with each other, because finding a babysitter for an out-of-control child is nearly impossible. So social interaction is out. Date nights are out. And the isolation deepens.

If the parents can stay on the same page—or even in the same book—the stress and alienation might be eased somewhat. However, if the child has effectively begun splitting the relationship, the isolation may intensify. Single parents are well advised to stay in touch with their support systems and relational circles in an effort to maintain some sense of psychological balance. Parents need to pay particular attention to the children who were in their home prior to the adoption, so they do not sacrifice the quality of parenting they had up to that point.

It is easy to become overwhelmed and overly focused on the squeaky-wheel kid, forgetting—at least momentarily—to meet the needs of the children in the family whose functioning is more typical. However, parents must remember to spend time with all of the children to avoid a feeling of isolation on the part of the kids who were there first.

They're feeling the changes in family dynamics as much as their parents are. It may seem that they have lost their once-happy parents, and they may hesitate to bring their friends home because their new sibling may do something horrendous or embarrassing. They may get angry or they may withdraw. In either case, they need attention.

Parents, therefore, have dual responsibilities: they must maintain the quality of parenting with the children who have been in the home while simultaneously trying to mitigate the stress that has emerged as a result of the new child. Balance, balance, balance! It's a formidable task, but it is essential for everyone as the family finds its way along the path to improved functioning and health.

Moving beyond trauma

Once the family clearly understands the new dynamic and recognizes the challenges faced by the in-place kids and the new addition, they will be better prepared to move forward in their quest to help the adopted child heal and grow. Parents should not hesitate to seek professional services when they feel they are unable to effectively manage their new undertaking. The wisest choice is to seek guidance from a mental health professional who understands the trauma that results from early childhood maltreatment, loss, grief, attachment, and adoption. With appropriate therapy that is family inclusive and family centered, the hurt child can begin to move forward, and when this occurs, the integrity of the family can be restored.

Andrew, age 17, had been in his adoptive family for about nine months when his parents, Jen and Mike, finally acknowledged that they simply could no longer exist on a day-by-day basis hoping that "tomorrow will be better." As this realization developed, they spoke with a representative from their adoption agency who recommended a support group for adoptive parents. Jen and Mike had intentionally avoided joining any type of support group, convinced they were perfectly capable of parenting Andrew without help. After all, they had been effective parents for their birth children, and they initially thought their problems with Andrew might be nothing more that an overreaction to the new kid on the block. But perhaps it was time to rethink their decision.

Jen and Mike had been somewhat held hostage by Andrew's extremely aggressive outbursts and physical abusiveness. Like most victims of trauma, they blamed themselves: *Maybe we're expecting too much, maybe we provoked him, maybe he would have been happier in another family, maybe, maybe, maybe.* After attending the support group for a few weeks and talking with other parents who shared similar stories, they finally gained some perspective. Encouraged by this new awareness, they decided to reclaim control of their lives and their family. Some of the other families recommended therapists, and they set forth to do what they'd hoped to do when they first adopted Andrew: help him become a healthy person.

When Jen and Mike brought up the subject of therapy with Andrew, he was understandably resistant—he'd had masses of earlier therapy that did nothing at all—but he eventually agreed to have an assessment. During the meeting with the therapist, Jen and Mike talked about what had been going on since Andrew was placed with them. They provided extensive information on his background, including significant details about the ongoing nature of his maltreatment by his birth parents, which had led child welfare officials to remove him and seek permanent custody.

It soon became clear that Andrew's early experiences with his birth family had eroded his development, impaired his capacity to trust others, and overall caused him to be in a chaotic psychological state. As a result, he failed to make adequate adjustments in foster care. Between his removal from the birth home and his adoption placement with Jen and Mike, Andrew had lived in ten different foster homes. Early trauma and multiple placements ultimately compromised his capacity to develop a secure relationship with his new parents and siblings.

After talking with Jen and Mike, the therapist spent time with Andrew. Because he was an adolescent, it was necessary to get Andrew's agreement to participate in therapy, and, to everyone's surprise, he agreed. As the therapist explored the teen's history with him, it was evident that Andrew's cognitive processes consisted of many thinking errors. In addition to contributing to his behavioral difficulties, this poor processing actually *caused* some of those difficulties.

Andrew was unable to make accurate predictions and he lacked cause-and-effect thinking. He habitually engaged in primary process lying—obvious lying—and he became aggressive with very little provocation. The behaviors he exhibited during his assessment confirmed everything that Jen and Mike had told the therapist.

Without really comprehending the nature of his commitment, Andrew agreed that he needed to make changes in his life if he was ever going to become a participating member of his family. Although he had no clue about what he might do to address his difficulties, he said he was willing to try just about anything. He entered into a verbal contract with his parents, and even though it was probably not 100 percent genuine, it was enough for therapy to move forward.

Andrew, Jen, and Mike began a process designed to address as many aspects of the boy's life as possible. The therapeutic undertaking would take a considerable amount of time, and it would have to examine issues that included loss, grief, trauma, sexual abuse, distorted thinking patterns, and attachment.

During the assessment, Andrew was pleasantly surprised. He had never before spoken with a therapist who seemed to know precisely what he was thinking and feeling. This one was different: no games, no drawing, no inane questions. If one more therapist asked Andrew: "How do you feel about that?" he was certain he would explode. In truth, he didn't ever know what that question meant. How the heck was he supposed to feel about being abused and tortured by his birth family?

This therapist was more direct and in charge. To Andrew's amazement, he actually seemed to know what he was doing. His other therapists seemed bored and not too interested in his life. Another major difference was the fact that this therapy involved his parents. His previous sessions were pretty predictable: his foster parents would drop him off, he would play Uno with his therapist for 45 minutes, then his foster parents would pick him up.

"I always wondered why anyone would get paid big bucks to play card games with a kid," Andrew later said. "And what do games have to do with losing a family, being sexually abused and beaten, and needing a new family?"

Over time, Andrew and his parents started to become a bit closer. His parents were less angry with him, they hugged him, and they treated him as if he was an important member of the family. Even though he continued doing "stupid things" (Andrew's words), he became aware that his parents' responses to him were changing. They stopped grounding him, taking his phone, and threatening him with all kinds of punishments.

"I wondered what was wrong with them," Andrew says. "I kept trying to figure out what they were plotting next."

But there were no plots. No hidden agendas. What was actually happening was that Andrew was finally beginning to reason— to psychologically monitor his behavior. Some cause-and-effect thinking, although very basic, was beginning to develop. Once progress started, it seemed to continue. Jen and Mike were very excited, but they kept their emotions in check lest they overwhelm Andrew with the extent of the elation they felt.

Many parents are so happy with their child's improvement in behavior that they panic him by revealing just how ecstatic they are with his changes. This panic often leads to regression and a re-emergence of negative behaviors, so it is best to err on the side of understatement.

After several months, Jen and Mike saw major progress, and even Andrew thought things were better. When he exhibited his old behaviors, he got over his hissy fits much more quickly. Even when their intensity was strong, his recovery time was shorter and the frequency diminished—which is precisely the goal of therapy.

The right therapy and the right placement

Effective therapy for families dealing with complex trauma must be foundational and relational. This means that all aspects must be examined and understood by both child and parents, and the focus must be on creating an atmosphere in which the child can change the nature of his relationship with his mom and dad. All therapeutic efforts must be directed at enhancing the relationships within the family and, unlike traditional therapy, there is no direct attempt to develop a relationship between the therapist and the child. The purpose of this type of therapy is to alter and strengthen the familial relationships that are permanently in place.

The deep psychological wounds that result from trauma *can* be overcome. The child with complex trauma disorder *can* recover if he is treated appropriately. Adoptive parents should expect to be an integral and active component of the child's recovery, because the difficulties that arise as the result of trauma cannot be treated effectively outside the family context. In fact, any attempts to do so will be met with frustration and failure. For children who do not end up in a permanent family, the likelihood of recovery is minimal, and it becomes even more likely that they, as adults, will repeat their own trauma with the families they create.

Professionals working with children who have reactive attachment disorder have known for years that the level of psychological damage due to trauma depends on several factors.

- The age of the child when trauma occurs.

- The quality of the child's attachment *prior* to the occurrence of trauma.

- The quality of the child's attachment *subsequent* to trauma.

If a child developed a secure attachment before his traumatic experiences, that attachment may offer him some immunity. Conversely, if the child's attachment was damaged early in life, he is more susceptible to suffer from complex trauma disorder.

Placement in a permanent, healthy family, followed by the development of a secure attachment to that family, can help ease the child's traumatic experiences. Because this has been proven time and again to be true, it follows that all efforts to help a child who has been traumatized should include a plan for him to live in a stable, safe, and nurturing family environment where his development will be propelled. Since the family context is so critically important, professionals should do all they can to help keep families strong after adoption.

CHAPTER 2

The Adoption Checklist

If you were to eavesdrop on interviews between aspiring adoptive parents and social workers, the parents' side of the conversation might sound something like this:

"My wife would make the world's best mother! It's really so unfair that she can't have children of her own, because she has so much love to give and she's really great with kids. We have three nephews, and she's always taking them to the mall and buying them toys and video games. They love to visit us and they're always telling her how much they love her."

Translation: The man's dear wife is generous and giving to the point of overindulgence. A child who has never known abundance will likely be overwhelmed and confused by her extravagance.

"It makes me so sad when I think about all the abused and mistreated children in the world. I just don't understand how parents can hurt their own kids, and I would never let that happen in my family. I'd honestly like to adopt as many children as I can—three or four, if that's possible. They don't have to be related to each other. If what they have in common is nothing more than the need for a safe, stable home, that's good enough for me. I'm a single working woman, but I don't require a partner to be a good parent."

Translation: She clearly thinks she can juggle her professional career and a cluster of abused children all on her own. It does not appear that she has given any thought to the painful baggage that these children carry, nor does she realize how much of her attention and focus will be required to settle them in. She has also grossly underestimated the power of a reliable support system. While it doesn't have to be a spouse, a compassionate sounding board is a critical part of the equation.

"Although I've never been a parent, I believe I can take on whatever challenges an adopted child presents. I'm well educated and street smart, so there's not much that gets past me. I understand that kids who've been traumatized need special help, but raising kids isn't rocket science. I had wonderful parents who did an admirable job with my sister and me, so I know what works. I'm a good, intelligent person, so it logically follows that I can be a good, effective parent."

Translation: In spite of the fact that he's very sure of himself, he has no idea what might be in store if and when he becomes an adoptive father. He's convinced that the good parenting skills his mom and dad demonstrated will be universally effective, and that's simply not true. Kids who come from a background marked by abuse must be parented in a completely different way than their emotionally healthier peers.

These three prospective parents express a strong sense of confidence in their ability to raise a child in spite of the obstacles, and they should be applauded for that. Their intentions are noble, and they truly believe they have what it takes to be the perfect adoptive parent. If conviction and determination were enough to create healthy adoptive families, all players in these scenarios would live happily ever after. But it just doesn't work that way.

As difficult as it is to acknowledge and accept, not everyone is a good candidate for being an adoptive parent. Some folks have more patience, stamina, and resilience than others, and the presence or absence of these qualities must be factored in before proceeding with an adoption plan. At the very least, parents must be willing to face the full spectrum of negative possibilities—however distressing and depressing they may be—before they move forward. A willingness to look at the realities of taking in a bruised and broken child is a fundamental requirement if successful integration is going to take place.

A traumatized child, no matter how young, is not a *tabula rasa* just waiting for a new mommy and daddy to imprint him with positive experiences. Instead, he has already been marked by abuse and/or neglect that can cause a host of difficult-to-deal-with behaviors. This history must be acknowledged and addressed by prospective parents if there is to be any hope of building a functional family, and there is absolutely no room for denial. What the child has been through is very real and very damaging, and pretending it never happened doesn't make it disappear—and it certainly doesn't make it better.

To maximize their chances of success, adoptive parents must see themselves as agents of change. It's perfectly fine to hold on to preconceived expectations of what parenthood will be like (as long as you don't come crashing down if the fantasies fall apart), but you must also acknowledge and address the child's negative experiences. While it might be difficult and seem nonsensical to keep the past in the present, it remains the most effective way to rise to the challenges that seem to suddenly pop up out of nowhere, again and again and again.

Is adoption right for you?

Some parents will have a harder time than others raising a traumatized child, and that's simply an observation, not a criticism. People have specific strengths and weaknesses that manifest in a variety of ways—not better, not worse, merely differently. It is better to discover beforehand that you do not have the temperament for adoption rather than being shocked and shamed by feelings of inadequacy after placement. At that point, the commitment to the child has been made and is not easily undone. What's more, a failed adoption is the last thing an abused child needs. It's likely that he is already feeling unlovable, and rejection by yet another family will reinforce that notion. Once you make the decision to adopt, it is in the best interests of the child for you to remain unwaveringly on that path.

So, who's good at this and who's not? Providing honest answers to the following questions is a good start toward finding out.

Do you take a child's bad behavior or
acting out as a personal affront?

In many cases, children who have been abandoned by their birth parents believe they are not worthy of being loved. After all, if the people who created them turned their backs on them, they must not have any value. This belief can be so firmly imprinted that a child will do everything he can to prove that it's true. He will behave badly to reinforce the notion, testing the limits at every possibility.

"I knocked the lamp off the table and broke it. Do you still love me?"

"I put a banana peel in the vent in my room and now there are ants everywhere. Do you still love me?"

"I took your bracelet off your dresser and hid it, and I refuse to tell you where it is. Do you still love me?"

The goal is to generate parental anger, which is either equated with love or used to reinforce the little one's belief that he is, in fact, unlovable.

When a child does something horrid and it appears to be intentional, it's human nature to take such offenses personally. Everyone knows that people are supposed to be nice to one another, right? Why would an adopted child be so rude to the parents who are trying to help him? Doesn't he appreciate his new and improved life? The answers, in order, are: no, because, and no.

Treating other people well is a learned behavior. When parents do it, their children mimic it. When they don't do it, neither do their offspring. When a child who has not witnessed and/or experienced basic respect is uprooted and deposited in a nice home with kind parents, he will not automatically become a kind person. He will push and test and act out just because he can. His new circumstances are alien to him, and it is very unlikely that he is going to demonstrate the kind of gratitude that will make you feel good about adopting him.

You will suffer needlessly if you take his acting out to heart, because the slaps in the face will be far too frequent and much too painful. It is therefore important to remove yourself from the equation—emotionally, at least—and be sensitive to what motivates the child. This is about him, not you.

Let's say you're married and you have a friend whose husband left her. She's hurt, angry, and insecure; she's worried about finances; she dreads the possibility of never finding love again. Her intense fears are driving her to behave in unsavory ways: badmouthing all spouses, including yours; insisting that you pay whenever you go to lunch together because, "You have someone to help out with money and I don't;" behaving desperately in her quest to find a new partner.

Do you get offended and lash out at her for being rude, nasty, and foolish? Or do you consider the bigger picture, take the high road, and disengage to a degree? Common decency dictates the latter choice, even though the temptation might be otherwise.

It is the same with children. They are often driven by something much bigger than a desire to please you and be considerate of you, and it will often get in the way. You must be willing to step aside when necessary and let the monster move past you. For a while, at least, behaviors such as lying, stealing, cursing, and hoarding may become standard as the child tries to find his place in his new home.

Dustin was four years old when he was placed with Deb and Angie. Born to an immature, easily distracted single mom who willingly released him to the foster system, he had grown used to not having his most basic needs met. He often went hungry while living in his birth home because his mother simply forgot to feed him.

From the day he moved in with Deb and Angie, food was an issue for Dustin. At mealtimes he would consume enormous amounts, frequently eating so much that he became sick. His moms began to limit his portions, but they soon realized that wasn't sufficient. When they discovered stashes of crackers, granola bars, and cookies under his bed, they made the decision to install locks on the refrigerator and cupboards.

"We knew he was stockpiling because he was afraid of going hungry again," says Deb. "We tried to reason with him, explaining that it was different in our home and that we would never fail to nourish him, but he just kept gorging and hoarding."

Adds Angie, "We felt terrible that we had to resort to such extreme measures, but Dusty's eating was completely out of control. It was a battle we couldn't win and we were tired of the fight, so we diffused the situation be making food unattainable on his terms. He was angry at first and he yelled at us a lot, accusing us of starving him. But we knew that anger was really directed at his birth mom, not us, so we let it slide. Dusty eventually got the message that there would always be another meal—it was something he could count on. The locks came off after a few weeks and his eating habits stabilized."

Resolution occurred relatively quickly and without major incident. But imagine if Deb and Angie had been offended by Dustin's behavior and continued to confront him about it.

"This movie sucks. It's really shitty." The words were uttered nonchalantly by Caroline, age nine, as she sat at home watching a comedy with her parents. Stephanie and Edward had adopted her two years earlier, and the issue of the child's foul language was ever present. Both Stephanie and Edward found it extremely disturbing, and they frequently hesitated to take Caroline to social functions because her cursing was such an embarrassment to them.

"Ladies don't speak that way, Caroline!" admonished her father, addressing the movie incident.

"I'm not a lady, I'm a little kid," she retorted. "Fuck you."

And so it went. Caroline cursed and her parents took away her computer. Caroline cursed and her parents yelled. Caroline cursed and her parents grounded her. Caroline cursed and her parents yelled some more.

"We're absolutely at our wits' end," says Stephanie. "No matter what Edward and I do or say, Caroline flatly refuses to clean up her language. We've done everything we can think of to get her to stop—we've punished her and tried to appeal to her sense of what's right and wrong—but nothing works. It's a regular occurrence now, and it's maddening. Last week when I was at the mall with a friend, I saw a T-shirt that read:

I KNOW I SWEAR A LOT.

1. I am very sorry.

2. I'll try to be good.

3. 1 and 2 are lies.

4. You can fuck off.

As offensive as I found it, I couldn't help but think it was custom-made for my daughter. Why does she keep doing this to us? It's so unfair!"

The operative words in Stephanie's statement are "to us." Clearly, she and Edward take Caroline's profanity as a personal affront. Since they believe they must be the ones in control of how their family functions, they refuse to back off. Without realizing it, they are giving their daughter a huge amount of control. With a simple utterance, she can turn them into red-faced screamers and hapless pleaders—desperate threat-makers and frustrated negotiators. The child seizes the power because her parents hand it to her, and she's smart enough to realize she can use it as a tool against them.

Adopted children often feel that they are at the mercy of everyone around them. They can be abused by the people who are supposed to love them, they can be moved from home to home without any say in the matter, and they can be plunged into situations that feel completely surreal. So, as in Caroline's case, when a great deal of power is deposited in their laps, they clutch it with a fervor.

The more upset Caroline's parents get about her language, the more powerful she becomes. If, on the other hand, they refused to make such a big deal about it, that power would be shattered. It's impossible to win an argument with someone who doesn't argue back, so what's the point? If admonished once or twice and then ignored, Caroline would likely let go on her own.

Lesson to Stephanie and Edward: choose your battles carefully. This one was a loser from the start.

How will you deal with truly dreadful and dangerous behavior?
A child who defies you and disobeys you is one obstacle, and it's a tough one to overcome, to be sure. But then there's the child whose behavior is downright criminal, and that's when things can start to get really scary.

When children begin to escalate their behaviors into dangerous activities, parents must shift their focus from treatment concerns to safety concerns. If they are at all in touch with their kids, they should be very good at gauging whether or not their fears are reality based. It is important that professionals pay careful attention to the concerns and fears identified by parents, since they may be called upon to help develop a safety plan or even make arrangements for an out-of-home placement. Safety must *always* be the number-one priority.

Sean, age 13, intimidated Jessica—his single, adoptive mother—at almost every turn. Although she felt threatened by him, child welfare professionals continued to minimize and downplay the seriousness of his cloaked threats. After all, he was still young and he wasn't all that big. Yet Jessica's fears felt very real, and she continued to suffer from interrupted sleep, hypervigilance, and ongoing worry.

Occasionally, she would catch Sean sneaking around the house at night, seemingly on a mission to accomplish something. It was that unknown something that was of greatest concern to her. While Sean had never set a fire, he did leave evidence of scorched pieces of paper lying around—almost a warning about what he could do while the rest of the family was sleeping. Sean's therapist shared Jessica's concerns, and he continued to report his feelings to child protective services. The organization's wish to keep the boy in the home seemed to outweigh the potential risk of his doing harm to his mother and his sibling. Over time, Jessica's fears escalated to the point where she was terrified to close her eyes at bedtime.

One night, as she was drifting in and out of fitful sleep, she suddenly awoke to find three small fires burning around the entrance to her bedroom. She was able to extinguish the flames quickly, but the incident made her more fearful than ever. When she finally regained a modicum of composure, she decided not to confront Sean until the next day.

The following morning, Jessica sent Sean off to school without mentioning a word about the fires. She then systematically called both his therapist and the social workers involved in Sean's case. Just as she suspected, the fact that Sean actually did something instead of simply threaten to was enough to activate the system. He was removed immediately and transferred to a closed residential setting. To this day, it remains unclear whether Sean will ever be able to return to his mother's home due to the threat he posed.

Fires, physical harm to self or others, sexual acting out, and sexualization of other children—these problems and more can be part of an abused child's repertoire. Prospective adoptive parents must honestly assess which issues they are prepared to face.

Do you believe that love conquers all?

Real life is not a romance novel. It is not a fairy tale. The good guys don't always win, and bad things happen to good people. When the sun sets on a particularly horrendous day, a hug from a loved one may feel pretty terrific, but it doesn't necessarily ease all the pain. While love is an essential component of a healthy life, it isn't an all-encompassing solution to every problem.

When prospective parents think about adopting a child, they often see variations of the same scenario. A sad, abused child sits alone—his eyes huge and pleading, his sweet little face etched with misery. His family has been mean to him, people who are supposed to love him have hurt him and all he wishes for is a loving mommy and daddy to come along and save him from his wretched plight. *Sigh. Won't you come soon and save me?* And so he waits.

In fact, the phrase "waiting child" is often used by foster and adoption agencies, because these two simple words tug at the heartstrings. But the truth is, the child isn't waiting. Not for you, not for anyone. He's more likely trying to figure out what he can do simply to make it through one more day.

At the age of three, Cameron was living with his birth mother and his 18-month-old half-sister, Amanda. Their mom was a practicing drug addict who frequently chose getting high over caring for her children. A third half-sibling had already been removed from the home by child welfare and was in a foster-to-adopt program.

Cameron vividly recalls watching his mother tie a piece of tubing around her upper arm to prepare for an injection. (His story was later corroborated by his birth mother, whose memory of that day is as real as her son's.) As she tightened the rubber with her teeth, he planted his fists on his hips and began to scream at her. "Don't, don't, don't! I hate you, I hate you, I hate you!" He had witnessed this ritual enough times to know that once the needle hit the vein, he would lose his mother for hours, even days. In addition to having to fend for himself, he would have to make sure that Amanda was fed and changed and kept safe.

Does it appear that this child had even the remotest opportunity to fantasize about getting a new, loving family? Did he have the luxury of wandering off into a quiet corner to wish and wait? For Cameron and other children like him, it's all about survival.

Children who have been neglected or abused need a lot more than love and sympathy. In no particular order, they might need things like counseling, special education, psychological intervention, occupational therapy, and medication. Parents must address issues such as feelings of loss and grief, separation anxiety, insecurity, low self-esteem, and dozens more. All the "I love yous" in the world will fall on deaf ears unless these problems are addressed and resolved. Love helps, but it does not heal.

Are you anti-meds?

Some parents simply do not believe in medicating children. Citing instances of inaccurate diagnoses and physicians who are quick to overprescribe, they draw a definitive line in the sand. No drugs. Not for my kid. Ever.

While their accusations often have merit, they are not universally true. What about the seven-year-old boy who cannot focus long enough to complete a homework assignment or finish a meal? What about the four-year-old girl whose rage is so out of control that she screams most of her waking hours?

Prescription drugs often provide solutions that make a world of difference. To be sure, it's a tough choice to make, but it's often the right choice.

Heather and Keith adopted Ben and Meghan, full siblings, when the children were two and three. Now four and five, both children require medication to get through the day. Initially, Heather was firmly against any type of drugs, convinced they were a cop-out. She believed that if she was a good mother and parented well, her kids would be all right. But then her philosophy changed. The following excerpt is from Heather's mommy blog.

> Managing Ben's medication has been a challenge from the be-
> ginning. When everything is working right, he has amazing
> days—but when things begin to fall apart, we have very, very
> long days. Since his body continues to grow and change, his
> medication has to grow and change with him. This year, after
> much frustration and a bit of desperation, we sought out a psy-
> chiatrist and found a wonderful counseling center. Not only
> does Ben now have the benefit of weekly therapy, we also have

an amazing doctor who has given me new hope for his future medication management.

   In addition, after much worry and consideration, we requested a referral for Meghan. She now receives weekly therapy and is seeing a psychiatrist. Although it was a very hard decision, we opted to put her on medication in the hope that it will help her cope better with preschool and with life in general. We continue to pray hard that we have made the right choices for both Ben and Meghan, and we will continue to pursue whatever help they may need.

Was it tough for Heather and Keith to make the decision to administer medication to their children every day? You bet. Do they admonish themselves for doing so? Not in the least. In this family's case, prescription drugs benefit the children, and the parents are carefully monitoring their little ones to ensure that changes in drugs and dosage are made whenever necessary.

   Says Heather, "The belief that it's bad to medicate kids is the one stereotype I wish people could get past. I worry daily about what the long-term effects of the meds might be, but I absolutely know what will happen without them—and that road is one I will help my kids avoid at all costs. We have also had such tremendously positive responses from medication that could not possibly be achieved with any other therapy."

   The bottom line: meds can work. No, they should not be prescribed arbitrarily. No, they should not be the first course of action. But when recommended appropriately and reviewed carefully, they can relieve an emotional burden for both child and parent.

   Eliza was adopted as an infant by Sally and Tim. Born addicted to cocaine, she was a difficult baby—constantly restless and irritable. As Eliza grew, so did her parents' devotion to her. They rose to each new challenge with unwavering commitment, seeking out specialists when their daughter required intervention with attention, language, development, and behavior. When Eliza was four, her therapist recommended medication for her severe mood disorders.

"I wasn't crazy about the idea of medicating my daughter," says Sally, "but the poor child was always so angry! I used to wonder how dreadful it must be for her to live inside that rage-filled little body. Tim and I discussed it, and we finally agreed it was a chance worth taking if drugs might help calm her."

From the moment she gave Eliza her first pill, Sally diligently watched her child for signs of change. Would the meds make a difference? Would they stabilize Eliza, or would she turn into a drugged-out zombie-child? Sally went from encouraged to anxious and back again, constantly questioning if she had made the right decision.

Three days after starting medication, Eliza walked into Sally's study with a beaming smile on her face. As she flung herself into her mother's arms, the three words she uttered said it all: "I happy, Mommy."

Have you thought about the effect adoption will have on all members of your family?

If there are no other children in your home, feel free to skip this section. But if you are planning to bring a hurt child into a family with children already in place, you might want to linger here awhile.

The addition of an adopted child affects everyone. It makes no difference if the other children in the family are birth kids or adoptees, if they're healthy and adjusted or fragile and struggling. The new child does not discriminate, and he shares his pain and dysfunction with parents and with siblings, with the weak and with the strong. It's not that he consciously sets out to make life miserable for everyone (although in some cases, that may be true). It's more about the fact that a traumatized child's pain is huge and cannot be contained.

Trey and Kevin adopted Samuel from Ethiopia when he was two. Their experience was a positive one, and four years later, they opted to try again. By this time, Samuel was a healthy, thriving child, adapting well to his school environment and developing strong social skills. He was liked by his classmates, and his outgoing personality positioned him as a leader, albeit a gentle one.

The decision was made to try to adopt another little boy from Ethiopia. Trey and Kevin hoped for a child younger than Samuel, since they felt he would make a good big brother and serve as a positive role model.

Elias was five when he became part of the household, and Samuel had just turned seven. From the very beginning, it was clear that the two boys had nothing more in common than their motherland. Elias had gone from his birth home to an orphanage to the home of relatives and back to the orphanage, and the multiple moves had left him feeling unwanted and unworthy. His demeanor was dark and brooding, and his tendency to manipulate others was profound. Samuel seemed uncomfortable around him and went out of his way to avoid anything but the most superficial contact.

One afternoon, Elias wandered into Samuel's bedroom, where the older boy sat on the floor playing with his toy cars. Fuzz, the family cat, was sleeping in a square of sunshine beneath the open window. Elias plopped down on the bed and watched Samuel for a while, then walked to the window and pushed out the screen, which then hung precariously by a corner. With an uncanny blend of speed and precision, he scooped up an armful of the metal cars and flung them out the window. They landed with a clatter on the hood of the BMW parked in the driveway below.

"If you tell on me, next time I'll throw your kitty out the window," sneered Elias as he hurried out of the room, down the hall, and into the sanctuary of his own bedroom.

Of course, Samuel was blamed for the scratches on the car. Of course, he pleaded his case. Of course, Elias insisted he'd been in his own room the entire time. Of course, Samuel wailed that he never wanted a brother in the first place. Of course, incidents like this one occurred repeatedly. It took years of individual and family therapy for Elias to acclimate to his new family—and just as long for Samuel to readjust.

"We took a risk and we lost," says Trey. "Elias turned our happy family into a madhouse, with blame flying everywhere. I never planned to spend such a huge chunk of my life in therapy, especially when my intentions were simply to help another kid who needed a good home. Never again."

Adds Kevin, "I think we've made a big difference in Elias's life, but I deeply resent what he did to Samuel. Our happy and confident little boy became fearful and wary, and now we're trying desperately to undo that."

On different levels, both men regret having brought a second child into their home. Because they didn't anticipate any problems, they were ill equipped to deal with Elias's acting out. Furthermore, they had not adequately prepared and protected Samuel from the fallout, so he became the innocent victim. If Trey and Kevin had thought it through carefully, they could have handled the situation far better—or might not have adopted Elias at all.

If there are other children in your home, you must carefully consider the answers to these questions before adopting.

- What if anything, will they gain by the addition of a new child?

- What might they lose?

- How will they react to the anger directed at their parents by the newcomer?

- What will their friends think, and how will they handle any criticism?

- How will they deal with their frustrations and anger with extended family members?

- How will they address school situations if the new kid has ongoing difficulties and their peers somehow hold them accountable?

- How will they react to comments about the new kid if it is a transracial adoption and other kids make nasty or racist remarks?

- If the birth order is changed by adoption, how might the kids feel about losing their position in the family hierarchy?

It's not just about you and the new kid. There are other lives to consider.

How much of your belief about adoption is rooted in myths?
The adoption arena is riddled with myths, so it's wise to research your beliefs before making assumptions that simply aren't true. The fewer surprises you have, the better off you'll be.

"We adopted a child from an orphanage in Poland because both my wife and I have Polish ancestors. Living with a family of the same heritage will make it easier for him to adjust."

False. Culture is what you grow up with; it is not genetically transmitted. A traumatized child from Poland is not less likely to experience the results of trauma if he is placed with a family of Polish descent. Children who have lived in orphanages are not coming out of an experience that is reflective of their country's culture. They are coming out of a culture of institutionalization.

"Children available for adoption from other countries are emotionally healthier than kids in welfare systems in the United States."

False. Trauma is trauma, no matter where it occurs. The results are the same regardless of whether it happened in New Guinea or New York.

"We really want to adopt a sibling group, because if the kids are placed together, it's more likely that things will work out better for all of them."

False. This is a philosophical perspective that is not rooted in truth. Of course, adoption professionals should evaluate the viability of placing siblings together, but it doesn't always work. In fact, it can have the opposite effect. Sometimes, children who have been raised together in a completely chaotic environment are not able to live together without re-enacting their trauma. It is not unusual for their shared experiences to keep them from making an adequate adjustment. What's more, families have reported that when one child does well, the others falter, creating a pattern of alternating successes and failures.

In some situations where siblings are kept together, the group must be moved from place to place due to the dysfunction of one of the children. When agencies decide to move three kids around when just one has problems, they are likely causing trauma for the two children who are making positive adjustments. It is counterproductive for professionals to move two kids who consistently do well simply to meet the politically correct position of placing siblings as a group. Philosophy should not guide practice. Instead, it should be dictated by wise professional insights and clinical theory.

"If we adopt a younger child, we stand a better chance of having a successful adoption."

False. Common sense would lead to the assumption that a young child is more likely to settle in than an adolescent, but everything hinges on pre-adoptive circumstances and trauma. An infant may have endured the effects of a stressful pregnancy or may have been exposed to brain-damaging alcohol. The adolescent may have come into care later in life, armed with sufficient life experiences that helped take the edge off the trauma he experienced. There are no guarantees that a little one will be an easier one.

Are you prepared for a series of ups and downs?

Perhaps the most predictable thing about adopted kids is their utter unpredictability. Just when you think you've figured him out— just when you've mastered the parenting techniques that actually work—the child becomes someone else.

Laura and Booker became foster parents to Rachel when she was five days old. Her birth mother used methamphetamines during her first trimester and was tripping on LSD when the baby was born. Because Rachel's Apgar score[2] was high, Laura and Booker immediately thought their new daughter would be fine, and they were joyous when the baby's adoption was finalized after only ten months.

The first few years of Rachel's life were relatively normal and uneventful, but when she entered preschool at the age of three, everything changed. Starting on day one, Laura received regular phone calls from the school's administrator telling her she had to pick up her daughter, "Right now!" Rachel, it seems, was a very angry little girl, and she released her rage by hitting, biting, and scratching her classmates.

Laura established a regular pattern of bringing Rachel home from school whenever the child's teachers demanded it. Invariably, the little girl was positively angelic upon returning home. She would follow Rachel around the house, happily offering her help with cooking, cleaning, and gardening. The next day, there would be more abominable behavior at school, and the good and bad behavior kept Laura on a constant roller coaster.

Can you handle that? Would the angelic hours be enough to offset the crazy ones? Only you know the answer.

Really—what are your expectations?

It is important to carefully examine your intentions when you decide to adopt. If you are trying to fill some sort of personal void, you're setting yourself up for disappointment. You should not adopt so your only son or daughter can have a playmate. You should not adopt because you have three girls and would love to add a little boy. Your expectations will likely go unmet, and it is not the adopted child's role to meet your needs in the first place. He can barely be who he is, much less become the manifestation of a pre-conceived fantasy.

As critical as what you expect from your adopted child is what you expect from yourself. Do you assume you will parent him in the same way that you parented your birth children? Do you think he will respond to you just like they have? Do you believe you can spontaneously jump into parenting without taking into consideration how your behaviors and interactions will be received by the adopted child?

Questions, questions, questions! As annoying as they might be, we cannot stress enough the importance of looking deep inside yourself and providing honest answers. Trust us when we say that any adopted child will be better served by parents who truly know what they're getting into and are fully prepared to face the challenges.

If you're not there now, it does not necessarily follow that adoption is out of the question for you. With some focused work, you may be able to make the personal and attitudinal changes that can better equip you for the undertaking. You can't force it, but it just might happen. After all, the human spirit is powerful, and determination is a mighty dynamic.

CHAPTER 3

Preparing for Your Adopted Child's Arrival

When parents are anticipating the arrival of a birth child, they joyfully focus on choosing a name, decorating the nursery, loading up on baby clothes and diapers, and childproofing their home. They shop for strollers, car seats, stuffed animals, toys, and all the other paraphernalia that is part of new parenthood. They don't have to do any research about the child's background, because they *are* the background. They usually don't have to take special classes on how to be a parent, and they certainly don't require any training on dealing with the special needs of a traumatized child. As all consuming as their preparation may seem, it's nothing compared with the process that adoptive parents must go through.

When you're adopting a child, the list of pre-adoption tasks can be horribly taxing, seemingly endless, and sometimes painful. While parenting in its most basic form may come naturally to you, there are many other issues that must be addressed before your new son or daughter takes up residence in your home.

Your child's medical history

When you have birth children, you know precisely the possibilities that their gene pool holds: tall or short, light hair or dark, brown eyes or blue. You know if there's a risk of attention deficit disorder, hyperactivity, asthma, or autism. You know if there's a history of heart disease, diabetes, epilepsy, or depression. If you're smart, you're well versed in the symptoms of any potential issues and you know what to look for. Odds are, you watch your child's development carefully, poised to take action should any signs arise that might be an indication of a problem.

When you adopt a child, however, information on his medical history isn't immediately at your disposal. How can you know what to look for if you don't know his family background? That's why it's so important to get as many details as possible about your adopted child's genealogy. Don't think of it as prying, although some critics might perceive it that way. In reality, it's a smart, responsible way to know more about the emotional and medical challenges your child might face.

Before Leslie and Ted signed the adoption papers for Max, age two, they repeatedly asked the county adoption agency for specifics on his birth family. Just as repeatedly, they were delayed and deferred.

"We're having a hard time accessing that data. Maybe tomorrow."

"We hope to have something for you by next week."

"It's looking like we can get our hands on that information by next month."

Despite their best efforts, Leslie and Ted were eventually told that details on their son's family medical history were simply not available. Contrary to their better judgment, they abandoned their efforts and moved their attention to finalizing Max's adoption, which was their top priority.

When Max was three, he began drinking water and urinating excessively. Although he was constantly hungry and eating more than usual, he started losing weight at a startling rate. Puzzled and near panic, Leslie made an appointment with Max's pediatrician. The child was diagnosed with type 1 diabetes and immediately sent to the hospital for stabilization of his blood sugar levels.

"I know there's nothing we could have done to prevent this," says Leslie, "but if I'd known in advance about the possibility of Max developing diabetes, I would have been far better prepared. I would have researched the disease and known what to look for and what to do. Instead, I completely freaked out, scaring my son in the process. Having relevant medical information upfront would have avoided a lot of alarm and anxiety."

It's essential to explore as much of your prospective adopted child's background as possible. Make noise. Be pushy (but polite). Don't take "no" for an answer. If you know that there's even the remotest chance that such data is available, don't stop until you get your hands on it. If, however, you discover that it truly is an impossibility—for example, your child was abandoned and his birth family is completely unknown—only then should you give up the fight.

The open-book approach

Your child's medical history is just one small piece of the information you should have at your disposal prior to adoption. Ideally, you should receive as much training and preparation as possible before the new child joins your family. The more knowledge you have, the better primed you are to deal with any problems that may arise.

It is imperative that professionals be completely truthful during the pre-adoption process. Sugarcoating any event or potentially tumultuous experience will only intensify the negative components of the activity and complicate it for others. If the adoption professional is honest, the prospective parents will have a clear picture of what they might expect, and they won't delude themselves by thinking that all will be sweet, loving, and perfect once placement occurs.

Pre-adoptive training must also emphasize that adoption is not just about family building. A hurt child is not a clean slate. He is not predictable. He cannot be molded into your ideal vision. As he walks by your side, holding your hand, he joins you on a venture into the unknown, and you need the benefit of a roadmap to prevent the journey from ending up hopelessly off track.

Prospective parents should be exposed to information on a host of possibilities. Might the child manifest temper tantrums, aggressive behaviors, hyperactivity, or self-abuse? Might he steal, lie, talk back, or beg? Will he be rude, noisy, seductive, or selfish? Is there a chance that he'll harm other children in your family or be cruel to your pets? Knowing the answers in advance won't remedy the problem, but at least you won't be caught completely off guard if a negative situation arises.

While honesty on the part of adoption professionals is critical, prospective parents, too, should be willing to open up about their concerns regarding adoption. They should be encouraged to do so without the fear of being judged, because worries and anxieties that are tucked into the back corners of the mind have a way of bursting out. Given the likelihood of the adopted child generating multiple surprises, parents certainly don't need any surprises of their own.

Lila was worried about adopting a child who had been sexually abused. As a young girl, Lila had been molested by a family friend. Although it was just a single occurrence, the mark it left was dark and deep. She never told Aaron, her husband, about the incident, so when they were given a checklist of problems that they would accept in a child, she followed his lead and agreed to consider one who had been sexually abused.

Ethan, age six, spent the first five years of his life in a highly sexualized birth environment. He and his two siblings frequently witnessed crude intimate behavior among the four adults in the home, and the children were often forced to be a part of it. Although he had been in therapy since his removal from the birth home, his preoccupation with sex became apparent soon after he moved in with Lila and Aaron.

It started with his drawings of male genitalia, which both his parents found extremely disturbing. It was therefore hardly surprising when Lila received a phone call from Ethan's teacher telling her that he had touched another child inappropriately. And that's when something broke inside her.

She was immediately taken back to that pivotal day in her own life when innocence and trust were replaced by betrayal and confusion. She began to shake uncontrollably, reliving the experience as vividly as when it first happened. Although she managed to drive to Ethan's school to pick him up, her emotions were still soaring dangerously out of control. She couldn't bear to look at him when he climbed into the car, and she drove straight to his therapist's office.

"I'm in the parking lot," she texted the doctor upon her arrival. "It's an emergency. Can you see Ethan now?"

Within minutes, he was standing beside Lila's car.

"He's acting out sexually in school," she told the therapist, fighting for composure. "Take him. I'll be there in a minute. I just have to call Aaron."

As soon as the doctor and Ethan were out of sight, Lila drove off.

Several miles later, she pulled over to the side of the road and called her husband. She confessed that she'd panicked and fled, and she asked him to pick up their son. Next, she left a voicemail message telling the therapist that Aaron would be by to get Ethan. Next, she resumed driving and didn't stop again until she had driven nearly 200 miles. Overwhelmed and terrified, she checked into a motel, called Aaron again, and told him about her own experience from many years ago.

"Ethan's sexual abuse was a reminder of my own," she explained, "and his acting out triggered all my old memories. I was afraid this would happen—that if we adopted a child who had been sexualized, the thoughts I tried so hard to squelch would come flooding back. I should have been honest when filling out the adoption questionnaire, and I certainly should have been honest with Aaron."

Ethan continued with his therapy and Lila started therapy of her own. Her greatest wish was that their shared experiences would give her a better understanding of what motivates her son.

"But frankly," Lila admits, "if I had to do it over again, I never would have put a check mark next to the 'sexual abuse' box. I believe I could have gone through the rest of my life without ever having to face my own abuse in therapy."

Honesty. It really is the best policy.

The home study process

One of the biggest challenges parents will face once they make the decision to adopt is completing the home study. The home study process—almost by definition—is highly judgmental. The questions asked, both in person and in writing, dig deeply into who you are, where you come from, and how you live your life. While the level of personal scrutiny is important, it does have a way of making parents feel inferior and inept. They fear they won't be good enough or be considered worthy of adopting a child in need.

Emma and Stuart wanted desperately to have a family. After years of trying, scores of medical tests, and several *in vitro* fertilization procedures, they decided to adopt. Because their finances were exhausted, they could not afford a private adoption that would enable them to have an infant. Instead, they hoped to be matched with a toddler through their local county's foster-to-adopt program.

"The paperwork alone was mind-boggling," reports Emma. "It went on for page after page, and some of the questions were so highly personal. Stuart and I had to dig into the backgrounds of our parents, too, and it all felt so invasive. I was sure we wouldn't qualify."

"We're good people," adds Stuart, "but after answering all those questions, I felt like I could never stack up. I was sure that every little thing I did wrong when I was in college would come back to bite me, that being a frat boy all those years ago would prevent me from becoming a father."

Emma and Stuart's concerns were unfounded. The agency placed Sofia, a two-year-old girl, in their care shortly after their home study was completed. And the little girl didn't give a hoot that her new daddy used to dress up in a toga and drink way too much beer during his sophomore year.

Our advice to prospective parents who are struggling under the weight of such intimate inspection is to understand that all of these questions are for the benefit of the child. Sure, it's not a perfect process. Sure, people can lie on the forms. But, in our opinion, it's a necessary evil. Like other discomforts that must be endured in the pursuit of something you truly want, this one's definitely worth it.

Facilitating behavioral shifts

In the course of their training and preparation, many prospective adoptive parents are led to believe that once the child is living in a permanent home, he will no longer have the difficulties he had in foster care. In fact, some adoption professionals go so far as to suggest that permanency may or *absolutely will* mitigate some of the child's maladaptive behaviors. Unfortunately, there is no hard evidence to support this. Where an individual resides does not alter his personality or temperament.

Certainly, a child who is not constantly on the move or always wondering if he will be moved again may become more settled. However, that fact alone will not remedy years of mistrust, hypervigilance, betrayal, abuse, and neglect. In some way, all of these characteristics have become a part of who the child is, and these features will not change simply by relocating him.

Parents should hope for shifts in difficult behaviors and emotions, and they should be prepared to work at facilitating new ways of living and thinking. But equally important, they should be aware that all members of the new family will have work to do—perhaps a lot of work. In many instances, it may require the support of a professional who can help guide the process of change.

Humans are creatures of habit: each of us has our own routine and our way of doing things. If you've ever undertaken the process of personal change, you have a clear—perhaps painful—understanding of the adage "old habits die hard." Think about how difficult it can be to start a weight-loss plan or an exercise regimen. Think of all the well-intended but unmet new year's resolutions.

Children, too, have their own habits, so it is safe to assume that almost everything you have heard about your adopted child's behavior will continue to take place in your home. If he's been rude and defiant, he'll continue to test limits. If he's always broken his toys, the reign of destruction will continue. If he has a reputation for being mean to other children, that aggression will stay the same.

Some people pooh-pooh this assumptive attitude, claiming it is unnecessarily negative. However, believing that a new home and family will suddenly result in a major behavioral overhaul on the part of the child is unnecessarily naïve and misleading. If you expect that the move to permanency will eliminate the problematic behaviors that have existed for years, you are doomed to disappointment, surprise, and perhaps dismay.

Placing agencies would be doing adoptive families a great service if they shared the likelihood that difficult behaviors will continue until there is a reason for them to cease. Furthermore, the child will need help to alter how he behaves. The parents are the primary agents of change, but as we keep pointing out, professional intervention is often necessary.

For several months, Bill and Joan had been visiting 12-year-old Vincent while he was living at his foster home. During their time together, they enjoyed going to ball games, the zoo, the amusement park, and the movies, and Bill and Joan were enjoying this first phase of their adoption journey. They saw none of the issues that they had heard about in their adoption preparation classes, and Vincent had not exhibited any of the problem behaviors that his foster parents had described. This came as a happy surprise to Bill and Joan, and they began to feel that they had been unjustifiably negative in thinking that Vincent was going to present difficulties in their family. Although they had received very good preparation from the child's caseworker, they hadn't noticed even a glimmer of the issues that they expected to surface.

Soon Vincent began spending weekends with Bill and Joan, and the first two went very well. Joan was becoming more optimistic about how things were moving along. They had expected to see the behaviors that were outlined for them—food hoarding, furtive sneaking around the house during the night, stubbornness, and temper tantrums—but there wasn't a sign of any of it. Bill and Joan were relieved by this, and started to think that maybe—just maybe—Vincent had changed his old ways.

The third weekend visit occurred over the Fourth of July, and Vincent was staying for three nights. Bill and Joan were hosting their annual picnic for family and friends, and they were excited that everyone would finally get to meet their new son.

The morning before the event, the family of three headed out to the local supermarket to stock up on the food they would need for entertaining. Bill had carefully planned the menu, but as they walked down the aisles, Vincent began asking for all kinds of food that weren't on the grocery list. Bill was happy to allow Vincent to make a few choices, but he wasn't expecting the boy to want nearly everything he saw.

When Bill put a clear limit on what he was prepared to buy, Vincent became incensed and even more demanding. As his voice became louder and more insistent, Bill suggested that Joan take Vincent out to the car and wait for him to finish the shopping. Vincent threw himself on the floor of the store and refused to leave, continuing his wailing at a deafening volume. After about

20 minutes—which is about 19 minutes longer than we would have endured—Bill and Joan physically carried Vincent out of the store and maneuvered him into the back seat of the car.

As they drove off, Bill glanced at Joan, who refused to return his gaze. Frustrated, baffled, and more than a bit angry, she felt at a complete loss. When the family arrived home, Vincent sullenly sat in front of the TV while his parents put the groceries away. Out of earshot of their son, Bill and Joan briefly discussed Vincent's behavior in the store.

"I guess this is what they told us about," remarked Joan, an edge of sadness to her voice. "It really caught me by surprise, because he's been so good up till now."

The rest of the day progressed rather smoothly and uneventfully, and the only real difference was that Vincent was less talkative than usual. The three ate dinner, watched a movie, and went to bed.

It wasn't long before Bill and Joan heard Vincent leave his bedroom and go downstairs. Alarmed at first, they were relieved to hear him return to his room about 20 minutes later. In the morning, however, that initial alarm turned out to be well founded.

The kitchen looked as if it had been raided by a bear. All the food they had bought for the picnic had been either consumed or flung wildly around the room. When Vincent wandered in a few minutes later in search of breakfast, Bill asked him about the mess. Predictably, the boy denied that he had anything to do with it. When Joan went to Vincent's room, she found wrappers and half-eaten food all over the floor. And suddenly things became eminently clear: since Vincent didn't get to buy everything he wanted at the store, he simply decided to trash what his parents had bought.

The scene was a huge wake-up call for Bill and Joan, who finally realized that they were not, in fact, the luckiest adoptive parents on the planet. The agency was correct when they warned Bill and Joan of behaviors such as the ones they had recently witnessed, and they were naïve to believe only what they experienced during Vincent's honeymoon period with them.

When Joan took Vincent back to his foster home after the holiday weekend, she had a long conversation with the boy's foster mother.

"I tried to tell you," the foster mom gently explained, "that Vincent has demonstrated serious food issues in our home for the past year. I'm sorry that what he did came as such a surprise to you, but it sounds very typical to me."

Instead of being angry, Joan felt relieved. She was finally seeing the authentic Vincent instead of the superficially compliant one. While some parents might have been put off by seeing the real (translation: difficult and troubled) kid, she was happy for this stark dose of reality. Together, she and Bill agreed that they could deal with whatever obstacles their son would present.

Fortunately, Bill and Joan had been adequately prepared for what they might expect from Vincent—in spite of the fact that they initially chose to ignore the advice. Once they stepped out of la-la land and into reality, they were able to regroup and tap into their pre-adoptive training to deal appropriately with the situation. An honest presentation of potentially problematic behaviors allowed them to manage more effectively their feelings about, and responses to, Vincent's unsavory behavior, and full disclosure provided them with some immunity to its impact. Had they been blindsided by not having received detailed discussions of Vincent and his problems, they may have overreacted to his stubbornness and destructive behaviors.

Consider the big picture

The mental health world seems to be obsessed with a focus on the strength-based model, which emphasizes stressing an individual's most favorable qualities and minimizing any pathology that might exist. While this perspective may have some usefulness, it clearly misses some very critical factors for prospective adoptive parents. In many cases, sharing only the child's strengths is misleading or even dangerous. In an attempt to be supportive and positive, agencies frequently gloss over problems that parents have a right to know about.

Imagine going to the emergency room with symptoms of a heart attack. Instead of addressing your possibly life-threatening condition, the doctor on call goes on and on about how great it is that you run five miles a week and don't eat red meat. And, oh, by the way, your eyesight is excellent, your hearing is amazing for someone your age, and your kidney function is great. *Um, but doctor, I'm in the middle of a heart attack here.*

When reviewing a child's strengths and weaknesses, a balanced approach makes the most sense. It allows parents to look at the big picture and decide if they can live with the negatives. There is nothing to be gained by withholding information that might be essential for parents to have.

Quinn and Eugene wanted very much to adopt Jerome, age eight. They contacted his adoption worker after they saw a flier about him at an adoption conference. They already had an approved home study, and they were eager for more information about the little boy.

They were told about his special-education needs, his sleep difficulties, and his roughness with the pets in his foster home. These issues all seemed as if they were ones they could deal with, so they decided to meet him and seriously explore adoption.

Quinn and Eugene spent afternoons with Jerome while he was in foster care and eventually transitioned to weekend visits with him at their home. On his sixth weekend, they awoke on Sunday morning to find several burned areas in the living room carpet. They were both surprised and alarmed. Obviously, Jerome had lit fires during the night, and the results could have been deadly.

They tracked down his social worker—after all, it was a Sunday—who begrudgingly shared that there had been one other incident of fire-setting in a previous foster home.

"But it happened just that one time, so we didn't think it was an issue," she said by way of explanation.

To say that Quinn and Eugene were upset would be an understatement. They were livid that they had not been informed about this critical piece of Jerome's history, and they felt betrayed by the adoption agency. Although they are still going through with Jerome's adoption, their anger runs deep.

"If we had been made aware that setting fires was a possibility—however remote—we would have been more vigilant," says Eugene. "Even if we couldn't have prevented it, I feel that we would have been more empowered if we had that information. If we had known what might happen, it would have made a huge difference."

The dangers of rose-colored glasses

Most adoption professionals would prefer that prospective parents have an optimistic outlook on the adoption process, on pre-adoptive training, and, most important, on the child they are considering adopting. Clearly, a positive view of life in general is a quality that healthy, well-adjusted individuals embrace. Looking at the world from a bright perspective helps people reframe those things that might otherwise be seen as negative and/or overwhelming. What's more, a positive outlook offers some emotional immunity when bad things happen.

No one would argue that parents who adopt an abused, baggage-laden child are not well served by optimism. However, when optimism obscures reality, it becomes non-productive and interferes with the ability to take a proactive stance to remediate the child's difficulties. Instead, parents must be able to adjust the way they see things in direct response to the circumstances they are in.

To view every situation through the same lens limits flexibility and may result in rigidity. If something bad is going on with the child, it must be perceived as bad. After all, how can you remedy it if you don't acknowledge it? Common sense, which is often far too uncommon, will serve adoptive parents well.

Except in emergency cases, almost all domestic adoptions begin with pre-placement visits. These visits facilitate the beginnings of developing relationships, and they should be consciously designed to do just that. The child will, in all probability, want to look good. Initially, he will most likely showcase everything positive that the parents have been told about him. In the same way, the parents will want to make a good impression on the child, so they may begin relationship-building in a manner that may not reflect how they will actually be living together as a family.

Many visits are completely fun-focused, with excursions to the zoo, the park, the water slide, or the kids' museum. While good times with your child are important, he may get the false impression that all your family does is play.

Wow! This mom and dad will be awesome to live with. They aren't like my foster parents, who made me clean my room, take out the trash, pick up dog poop, and mow the lawn. These guys eat out all the time, and they don't even care if there are any vegetables on my plate. It's gonna be pizza, hot dogs, and French fries forever. What a deal! So, how soon can I move in?

Simultaneously, the parents might be thinking, *He is so much fun and easy to get along with. He eats everything he orders in a restaurant, and he gets so excited when we go somewhere. At the amusement park, he ran from ride to ride with a lot of enthusiasm. He talked with the other kids and was so friendly and compatible. When we got home quite late that night, he even went to bed without arguing.*

What the child and parents fail to see is that these visits are not reflective of typical day-to-day living. When overly entertained during pre-placement, the child is disappointed after he moves in and discovers that it's not all fun and games every day. There are chores to be done, meals—with vegetables!—eaten at home, and boring visits with aunts and uncles.

Prospective adoptive parents should attempt to plan balanced visits that are similar to how life will be after placement. Of course, it makes perfect sense to have fun on some of the visits, but it should be the sort of fun that is typical of the family. If you never, ever go to the beach because you burn at the mere thought of time in the sun, don't take your child there and lead him to believe that he can expect more of the same in the future.

If the child is of school age, it's a safe assumption that he will already have developed personal preferences about a lot of things: games, toys, electronic entertainment, food. Obviously, you should be open to exploring his interests and should attempt to accommodate whatever you can and whatever you feel is appropriate.

As you create this balance of fun and responsibility, it is important to keep in mind that your new child may not know how to perform simple household chores. Making his bed and loading/unloading the dishwasher may be completely alien to him, because he may not have had his own bed or ever laid eyes on a dishwasher. These are tasks that can be easily taught. Just make sure you don't express incredulity or even sympathy over his lack of knowledge.

"Here, let me show you how to do the corners when you make your bed."

"Loading the dishwasher is pretty easy. The plates go here, glasses there, and silverware in that rack."

Keep it simple and matter of fact. He'll learn in time.

Rules and rigidity

During the adoption preparation process, prospective parents should take a careful and critical look at what they can and cannot manage to live with. Some families are very set in their ways, as seen in the following proclamations.

- "We don't *ever* eat fast food."

- "I would *never* allow my teenager to have that kind of haircut."

- "No six-year-old will talk to me that way!"

- "We don't use foul language in our house."

- "I won't tolerate lying."

- "My child would never dress like *that*!"

Value systems are useful, to be sure. But the more defined a family is by rules such as those listed above, the more difficult it is to raise a child who has come into your home after trauma and multiple placements. This is not to suggest that families should embrace an anything-goes mentality, but rather to determine what you can and cannot live with in terms of the child's habits and behaviors. If your requirements truly are inflexible, adopting a child with special needs may not be the best choice for you.

Tony, a single adoptive dad of a 14-year-old, initially thought he could parent an adolescent with psychological difficulties and also change the kinds of choices his son made.

"I was firm in my belief that certain things could not and would not happen in my home. I am a moral person who does not steal, lie, or betray the people I love. I assumed that this would, somehow, be transmitted to my adopted son. Who did I think I was? I am a mere mortal—not a magician. How could I have been so naïve as to think I was capable of transforming another human being?

"In reality, I had no choice about many of the decisions that Zachary made. My role was limited to deciding how I could respond to and deal with his stuff. Since I love Zachary and never considered dissolving the adoption, I entered an unfamiliar world—his world. It was filled with a vast array of new acronyms, meetings, probation officers, warrants, therapists, and incredible pain. I never thought that loving my son so much could hurt so much.

"I was sad about his shame and pain, and I was fearful for his future. I stayed close to him, sat in multiple courtrooms, and watched him become so much more like his birth family than my family. Sometimes, I wondered why all of this didn't make me mad at him. But a special relationship had developed between us—a relationship that allowed for love and forgiveness and an unending sadness about the trauma that shaped his life.

"Zachary is an adult now, and while he has some difficulties, he has become a decent young man. Even more important, we have a wonderful relationship, and I cherish that with all my heart."

Part of preparing for a child or adolescent to join the family requires an introspective journey. How comfortable are you with the thought of not having control over a major part of your life? How will you feel when your hopes and expectations vanish? What will it be like for you when your nieces and nephews are going off to college or the military while you're on your way to court with your kid? What will you do if your daughter decides to reconnect with her birth family after years of creating turmoil that you endured in the hope of having a future with her?

Questions like this could go on endlessly, and they are not intended to be negative or to dissuade you from adopting. Instead, they are intended to make you think about what you might experience and to determine how you feel about the possibility of finding yourself in the midst of extreme behaviors and circumstances. Are you ready to walk side by side with the person you adopted, no matter what? Are you ready to pick him up and dust him off when he stumbles—accidentally or on purpose? Are you aware that adopting a hurt child requires a lot of work?

We assume that everyone thinking about adopting has already considered the positives. We want to give you the complete picture and encourage you to consider the less-than-perfect possibilities.

We are not saying that bad things *will* happen—merely that they *may* happen. When the coastguard tells boaters that everyone on board must have a lifejacket, they are not saying, "You will capsize or fall overboard and you will probably drown." They are saying, "Just in case you need one, take one."

International adoption

Most parents who are adopting internationally do not have the advantage of pre-placement visits. Each sending country has a different twist on how much contact the new parents have with their child prior to returning to the country where the parents live. Some countries send infants with escorts, and there is no contact prior to placement. Other countries, such as Colombia, require families to spend six to eight weeks in the country before they go to court to legalize the adoption. In these cases, families have the opportunity to spend time together.

In most cases, however, children leave the orphanage, get on a plane, and head home to a different world with new parents, an unfamiliar language, strange food, and many unknowns. The preparation is minimal, to say the least. Talk about trauma! Most adults would experience tremendous stress and anxiety if they were immersed in a new culture surrounded by people who do not look like or sound like them.

If you are undertaking an inter-country adoption, consider taking photos or videos of the orphanage and the orphanage staff to share with your child later on. Most children have some interest in where they came from, and anything that you can do to help fill in the blanks will be extremely useful as questions emerge.

Many times, internationally adopted children have no information about their birth families. In fact, they may have no family history at all. If they were abandoned, the slate remains completely blank, and they often have invented birth dates. This lack of information causes significant post-adoptive stress for many individuals.

These initial deficits are usually not insurmountable, but parents need to realize just how huge they can be. Children who are adopted in their own countries may have some possibility of reconnecting with birth relatives at some point, but international searches can be very difficult.

In such situations, parents should be prepared to learn as much as they can about the child's country of origin and the reasons why so many children in that country are available for adoption. Armed with this data, they can help create a narrative for the child. It is essential to clarify for the child that this is not his personal story, but rather a composite that likely comes close to the reason why he was in an orphanage and why he was available for adoption.

Creating such a narrative will enable the child to answer questions from people who will, inevitably, ask about the circumstances of his adoption. When people—both adults and children—realize that someone was adopted, the questions start. If the child can respond with something other than, "I have no idea. I don't know anything about the country I was born in," he will be better prepared to face the often-inappropriate questions that are guaranteed to come his way.

Andrea and Jack adopted Jiao from China. When she was old enough to understand, they explained to her, "Since someone found you all alone on a train wrapped in a blanket, your birth parents probably weren't able to keep you. But they must have wanted you to be safe and to be found by someone who would take you to an orphanage so that you would be okay.

"When you were born, many parts of China had a rule that said families could have only one child, while other parts allowed parents to have two. Many families preferred to have boys who could work on the farms and inherit money and property. Maybe your parents already had a son whom they loved, and they didn't want him to leave the family since he had been there for a while. Or maybe they had a girl and wanted a boy, and when you were born, they decided to do something that would help you have a good life with another family.

"Many Chinese women who were pregnant at the time you were born were talked into having an abortion. In your case, your birth parents wanted you to have life. No one knew exactly when you were born or what you were called, so the people in the orphanage guessed about a birthdate and gave you the name Jiao. It means dainty and lovely, and that's exactly what you are. We're sorry that we have to guess about so much of your early life, but that is all we can do since we don't really know too much at all. Just know that we love you and feel blessed to be your parents."

Such a narrative will help Jiao feel as if she knows something about where she came from, what her story might have been, and how and why she ended up in another family in another country. When people ask her questions, she will feel more comfortable being able to say something instead of having to invent answers on the spot.

Transracial adoption

Many adoptions, both domestic and inter-country, are transracial, generating additional issues that must be prepared for. Race is a critical issue in most societies, and adoptive families need to be able to talk about it with their children in an open, comfortable manner. Mixed-race families will inevitably face a barrage of questions in their neighborhoods and schools, so preparation is key. Keeping responses short and simple is the best way to handle it.

In same-race placements, outsiders do not immediately know that an adoption has occurred or that anything is different about the family until someone brings up the subject. In transracial adoptions, however, people can immediately see that the family is not a birth family.

Parents who believe "we are all the same" do a disservice to their children who are of a different race. The truth is—we are not all the same. Our packaging is our initial presentation to the world, and it's what people notice first: things like gender, race, height, and weight. Therefore, parents must be able to discuss race and its unique distinctions. Avoiding these conversations will usually make the child feel uncomfortable—akin to not talking about the elephant in the middle of the room.

Transracially adopted children and adolescents often wonder how they will fit in, and they are sometimes concerned that if they are seen in public with their families, they might get teased about having parents who are a different color. While this cannot be prevented—people can be very thoughtless—parents should attempt to balance the situation by providing a mixed-race environment to allow for interactions with a diversity of people. The adopted child will feel less racially isolated if he has contact with others who are like him. Kids who grow up exclusively in a racial group that differs from their own often have intensified identity struggles in adolescence and adulthood, and they frequently end up trying to be *more* of what they are—more black, more white, more Asian—and frequently become a parody of their race in an attempt to compensate.

If a family does not live in a racially diverse community, they should make whatever effort they can to expose their child to people of his own race, and they definitely must have ongoing communication about race and race-related issues.

Mark and Shandy decided to adopt from Ethiopia, and they came home with a five-year-old boy whom they named Adam. They lived in a small rural town in the Midwest, and there were no other people of color in their part of the state. As Adam grew up, the family experienced no obvious issues related to race, and there was little to no discussion of racial matters. Adam had a lot of friends, was always invited to birthday parties, and frequently had sleepovers both at his home and the homes of his friends.

Adam did well in school, participating in various sports and serving on student council. In addition, he was active in his church's youth group. When he was in ninth grade, he decided to invite a girl named Ellie to the homecoming dance. He was good friends with her brother, and he had known her for most of his life. Ellie was thrilled about the invitation to the dance, and she told Adam that she would ask her parents. Over the next few days, however, Ellie avoided Adam at school. When he finally caught up with her and asked her if she had talked with her parents, Ellie's gaze shifted to the floor as she told him she couldn't go to homecoming. Adam nodded awkwardly as he walked away. He was surprised and disappointed, since he had assumed that everything would be fine.

When Adam returned home after school, his mother noticed that he was especially quiet and seemed a bit sad. When she asked him what was bothering him, he told her about his letdown. Shandy was concerned, but since she knew Ellie's mom, Becky, well, she decided to give her a call and ask about the situation. When she talked with Becky, she could tell that there was a level of discomfort with the topic. Ultimately, Becky said that while she adored Adam and had for years, she just didn't believe in interracial dating. The conversation grew increasingly uncomfortable, and the two women abruptly ended the call. Shandy was stunned. She and Mark had known Ellie's family for years, and there was never any indication of discomfort with issues of race.

Shandy decided to address the situation with Mark when he came home from work. They had never discussed race, and, for the most part, they had not given the topic any significant thought. After Mark and Shandy talked, they knew they had to have a serious chat with Adam. It would be difficult to visit an issue that had remained unspoken for the boy's entire life. What would they say? How could they say it? They knew Adam would feel very hurt, and they reflected on how ignorant they had been not to have approached this topic much earlier.

Had there been open discussions about race and the various kinds of issues that might arise, this difficult situation would have been easier to manage. Once again, the importance of comprehensive pre-adoptive preparation cannot be overstated. Opening doors early will make addressing problems much more efficient and effective.

CHAPTER 4

Trauma: A Potentially Transferable Condition

Many people who adopt also have other children in their homes—either by birth, adoption, or foster care. In her book, *Welcoming a New Brother or Sister through Adoption*[3], adoption professional and psychotherapist Arleta James refers to these youngsters as "resident children." Some prospective parents spend significant time thinking about how adding a child or sibling group will affect their other children. Conversely, others do not take much time at all to prepare themselves or the resident children for the new addition, only to find, retrospectively, that these latecomers have forever changed the lives of everyone in the family. Some of the changes may be positive, and some of them may negatively affect everyone.

A child who has experienced trauma carries around the effects of that trauma like unwanted, unnecessary, but very real baggage. He cannot check it at the front door of his new home, although that would be a welcomed opportunity. Like a soldier returning home from war, the abused child brings "stuff" right across the threshold with him, and it is automatically shared, transferred, and subsumed by the people with whom he lives. It is not possible to set the trauma aside and go on with life as it once was. Instead, everyone in the household experiences a shift in the family system. These shifts are neither comfortable nor familiar, but they become the new face of the family.

For the traumatized child, a new family does not automatically mean a new life. In most cases, it means that the old life simply moves into a new family, whose members are probably not prepared for the aftermath of early sexualization, physical abuse, or profound neglect. Certainly, the resident children will have no idea how the introduction of trauma will upset the family, and they may not anticipate any difficulties whatsoever. How could they be expected to know what chaos might transpire, particularly if they have had no, or minimal, preparation?

To the resident children, their once tranquil, predictable family—complete with happy, responsive parents—suddenly turns into a minefield. Gone is the laughter, the loving, and the lightness of spirit. In its place are wariness, fear, and a tentativeness that never existed before. To compound the situation, the squeaky-wheel rule may kick in, causing the resident children to lose the attention of the parents. When the focus is shifted exclusively to the new child, the other children develop anger, resentment, and confusion. And their feelings are absolutely justified.

Caryn and Jim had two children by birth. When their friends adopted a child from an orphanage in China, they began to consider seriously the prospect of parenting another child. The more they talked to their friends about their new experiences, the more the intrigue grew. They often saw the adopted child, a ten-year-old boy named Kai, at church and church-related activities, and he seemed quite happy and well adjusted. Their two daughters—Shay, age seven, and Hannah, age six—liked to play with Kai even though he was a bit older.

As time passed, Caryn and Jim became more and more comfortable with the idea of adopting a child from China. They contacted the agency recommended by their friends, and then completed a home study and the necessary pre-adoptive training. They learned that most of the children who were available for adoption were boys who were older than their daughters. Since Shay and Hannah got along so well with Kai, the age issue didn't seem to be much of a concern.

Caryn and Jim discussed several children with their social worker, and they finally settled on a nine-year-old boy named Bojing. Abandoned by his parents because of a cleft palate, he had been living in the orphanage since he was born. Caryn and Jim felt that they could have the necessary surgery to repair his cleft palate performed in the United States and that Bojing would fit in perfectly with their family. Excited about their decision, they flew to China and returned with their new son, whom they nicknamed Bo.

Within just a few weeks, Bo began to act strangely. At about the same time, all sorts of things—the girls' toys, kitchen knives, and an assortment of seemingly mundane and useless items—went missing. In addition, Bo started to be very mean to his sisters, a fact that Caryn attributed to his upbringing in a boys' orphanage and his non-existent interaction with girls up to that point.

Shay and Hannah began to complain about their new brother, and Caryn tried to help them understand about his troubled past. Too young to comprehend the difficulties their brother had experienced, they weren't buying any of their mother's rationale. They didn't care that Bo had endured a grim start in life. All they cared about was having their Barbies' heads back on.

An insidious dynamic was at play. Because of his early trauma, Bo brought hypervigilance into his new family. His stealing and stockpiling for anticipated, non-existent emergencies was a reflection of that, and it caused his sisters to become hypervigilant, too.

The shift the family experienced was so severe that everyone needed to enter therapy. Caryn seemed to witness more of Bo's problems than Jim did, which caused marital stress. The girls were frustrated that their mom was more irritable than she had ever been. This wasn't the family that had been happy and carefree. This was a family that had become tense and watchful. The girls began hiding their toys and locking their bedroom doors. Behavior that was highly unusual for the family had become the new normal.

Therapy helped somewhat, but the going was slow and the frustrations continued to mount. Everything had changed. Caryn was busy attempting to arrange medical appointments for Bo in anticipation of his cleft-palate surgery, which cut into the time she could spend with Shay and Hannah. Jim's out-of-town travel increased—probably not by accident—and Caryn continued to feel isolated and somewhat helpless. She found herself thinking: *What have we done? Why can't I manage this situation more effectively?*

I feel so bad about all of the time the girls are losing out on. Her negative thoughts rambled on and on, compromising her ability to cope.

Finally, after about six months of therapy—which focused on Bo's early trauma, abandonment, and losses—Caryn and Jim felt some sort of shift back to a more balanced existence. Their son's troublesome behaviors were diminishing in frequency and he was bouncing back to normal a little bit faster. The girls' hypervigilance lessened, as well, since the incidents of stealing had tapered off. As additional time passed, the contented family of five that Caryn and Jim had wished for finally became a reality.

Caryn and Jim's story is not uncommon, but not all of these tales have the same happy ending. Many families flounder for years before finding the appropriate solution. Sadly, many never find the help they need, expending precious time and energy trudging through years of the wrong therapy and scores of revolving therapists. The result is often residential treatment or even adoption dissolution, because the structural shift is just too much for some families to manage. What's more, adoptive parents frequently find little or no support from their peers and families, who may not understand or even believe them when they try to explain what has happened as a result of the new child. Many hurt kids look very good to people on the outside of the immediate family.

If mothers, fathers, and resident children were prepared for the strange new world of adopting an abused child, they would be better able to sustain the intensity of the storms and the height of the waves. Placing a veil over the truth does not soften the effects of the mayhem that is likely to occur when a traumatized child moves into a new family. There is nothing—absolutely nothing—to be gained by not facing the negative possibilities with eyes wide open.

Choosing the right therapist

When dealing with the often-contagious problems of traumatized adopted children, it is important to seek appropriate therapy. This is something we addressed in Chapter 1, and it bears going into greater detail. Keep in mind that not every therapist is suitable. Not every therapist is effective. Heck, let's go for total honesty here (since we're touting it so much) and say that not every therapist is good at what he or she does.

Therapists are just like plumbers and teachers and electricians and veterinarians—some perform their jobs far better than others. The difference is that the average person is conditioned to think of therapists as a special breed of can-do-no-wrong professionals, and that is simply not true. In some cases, a therapist who knows nothing about the issues specific to adoption can cause more harm to a family than no therapy at all.

Claudia and Craig adopted Ashleigh when she was four years old. Left alone in an apartment for days at a time, she was removed from her birth mother when a neighbor reported the child's incessant cries. Claudia and Craig struggled through a year of Ashleigh's defiant and oppositional behavior, convinced that they could manage parenting without intervention. When the situation was clearly not improving, they opted to try the services of a child psychologist.

Because they had no idea where to turn, they sought advice from the director of Ashleigh's preschool. She recommended a therapist who had previously worked with two young brothers at the school who were both diagnosed with attention deficit disorder. The boys were currently doing very well, so she gave the referral without thinking it through.

While the director's willingness to help is admirable, attention deficit disorder is not complex trauma.

Dr. Madler was a pleasant man with a kind demeanor, rumpled clothing, and a beard à la Sigmund Freud. There were lots of diplomas and credentials on the walls in his waiting room, while toys and stuffed animals lined the shelves in his office. He had the right look. He had the right accouterments. But he didn't have a clue about adoption.

Claudia and Craig chatted with Dr. Madler while Ashleigh appeared to distract herself with a bear she'd pulled down from the shelf. So eager were they for a solution that they presented him with a written list of behavioral problems they'd been dealing with since the child's placement.

1. Avoids our hugs and kisses, but eagerly shows affection to strangers.

2. Lies constantly, even when it doesn't serve her at all.

3. Demonstrates no self-control.

4. Has trouble making and keeping friends.

5. Is controlling and manipulative.

6. Behaves aggressively and sometimes violently, especially with the cat.

7. Doesn't seem to trust us.

If Dr. Madler knew anything about adoption and trauma issues, he would have immediately recognized these as classic symptoms of attachment disorder, which is prevalent among adopted children who have been abused prior to adoption. But he didn't know, and so this is what he had to offer.

"You just have to loosen up, Mom and Dad," he began. (Note: If any child-centric professional calls you "Mom" or "Dad" instead of by your name, that's your cue to get up and walk out.) "Ashleigh is still adjusting to her new home, and your expectations of her are extremely high. Just give her more time to settle in and everything will be fine. In the meantime, I think you would both be well served by taking a series of parenting classes so you'll learn how to calm down and stop second-guessing everything she does."

So there you have it. In his "educated opinion," Ashleigh's behavior was her parents' fault.

Next, Dr. Madler said he wanted to spend some time alone with Ashleigh. Claudia and Craig had the presence of mind to refuse, so he ushered them aside and pulled a chair next to his for the little girl. Before he even said a word, Ashleigh did what she did best.

"I don't think Mommy and Daddy really want me to live with them," she said in a sad, tiny voice. "They always yell at me, even when I haven't done anything wrong. How can I make them love me?" She punctuated her words with a single tear that trickled purposefully down her cheek.

Dr. Madler looked at Claudia and Craig as if to say, "I told you so," but they weren't having any of it.

"Didn't you read number five on our list?" asked an exasperated Craig. "Manipulative? Controlling? Sound familiar?"

Added Claudia, "Can't you see she heard every word you said to us, then parroted it back in an attempt to prove that you're right and we're wrong? Who's in charge here, doctor? It's certainly not you."

But the angrier they became, the more convinced Dr. Madler was that they were the source of the problem. (Angry, red-faced parents do have a tendency to look guilty of *something*.) He told them he would like to see Ashleigh twice a week, and then dismissed them with a brochure on parenting classes. Of course, they never went back.

Claudia and Craig were savvy enough to recognize that, for all of his good intentions, Dr. Madler was essentially clueless. He fell right into their daughter's trap, and he would have languished there for months if they'd allowed it. Eventually, they contacted an adoption support group and were referred to a psychiatrist who specializes in attachment issues. Before just a few months went by, they could already see improvements in Ashleigh's demeanor. The road would be a long one, but at least they knew they were moving in the right direction.

But think of all the parents who believe unconditionally in the righteousness of therapists. They would have blindly accepted the doctor's assessment that they were at fault, and years could have been wasted pursuing the wrong solution. When making the critical decision to involve a therapist, make sure he or she is an expert in the adoption arena.

Going from bad to worse

The Attachment and Bonding Center of Ohio (Dr. Keck's organization) sees families from the United States as well as from several other countries, and the therapists there have met with many families whose experiences are similar to the case histories mentioned previously. They have heard horror stories about people's interactions with numerous kinds of professionals—

teachers, therapists, and coaches—who are frighteningly off base in their assessment of the adoption situation. Some families have seen as many as 40 different therapists before finding appropriate help, which is a terrifying reality.

It's not difficult to imagine just how frustrated parents become as they wend their way from professional to professional, all of whom seem to focus on *them* as the source of the child's dysfunction. How nice it would be if someone would actually acknowledge them as the potential resource for helping the child recover from the hurt and pain that early maltreatment caused! The following stories may seem unbelievable, but, with the exception of altering identifying information, they are all absolutely true.

Camille, age 12, was driven to cut herself. Her parents went to great lengths to protect her, locking up everything that could possibly be used as a blade. When Camille felt that she was old enough to shave her underarms and legs, her parents were worried about how to handle the situation. They decided that the safety razors they offered her wouldn't pose a threat, but ever-resourceful Camille dismantled the razor and proceeded to slash her legs. At that point, her parents decided that she couldn't be trusted even with so-called safety razors, so her quest for hair removal came to an abrupt end.

Never one to be outmaneuvered, Camille found a sympathetic guidance counselor at school who agreed that it was terrible to be saddled with such strict and controlling parents. The counselor, without any discussion with Camille's mother and father about their reasons behind the shaving restriction, gave the girl a safety razor so she could be just like the other girls in her class. Not surprisingly, Camille proceeded to cut herself. As the information unfolded, her parents were surprised (*Where on earth did the razor come from?*), shocked (*Will this child ever stop?*), and angry (*Oh, counselor, you are in serious trouble!*)—in that order. However, when they approached the principal of Camille's school, fired up by their fury, they appeared to be rigid, controlling, and more than a bit enraged. Although the principal agreed that the counselor's actions were unwise and irresponsible, he took no action. His only move was to suggest to the counselor that she stay in close contact with Camille's parents, who appeared to be ticking time bombs, for the safety and well-being of the girl.[4]

Dominic, 14 years old, had been sexually abused early in life by his birth parents and siblings. He became highly sexualized, and his adoptive parents, Olivia and John, always had their radar turned up high to identify any potentially charged situations that they felt he should avoid. Although it was embarrassing, they informed people at his school and at their synagogue that he should never be unsupervised around younger children.

Olivia and John had never felt comfortable about leaving Dominic at home with his younger siblings, even for short periods of time. After a few months in therapy, their psychologist felt that the teen might benefit from being treated like other adolescents. He explained that most 14-year-olds are capable of being home with their siblings without parental supervision. Furthermore, since nothing sexual had ever occurred in their home, perhaps demonstrating their trust in Dominic might help him develop more trust in them in return.

Although Olivia and John were extremely reluctant to comply, they caved in deference to the therapist's recommendation and decided to give normalizing their home a try. They took a brief trip to the grocery store and were back home in less than an hour.

Later that evening, their ten-year-old son, Timothy, told his parents that Dominic had shown him "bad pictures" on the internet. While nothing physical had happened, Dominic's trauma had been bestowed on his younger brother. This, of course, heightened the parents' vigilance and caused Timothy to trust his brother even less than he already did. Dominic was furious that his brother told on him, and, of course, he denied everything. When John checked the browsing history on the family computer, he found exactly what Timothy was talking about. Olivia and John felt betrayed by their therapist, and they also felt quite imprudent about not trusting their better judgment.

Anticipating problems—whether they're real or not

Parents of abused children often find that they start second-guessing many more things than they once did, which is yet another example of transferred trauma. Joshua, adopted at the age of eight, was a chronic thief, so when his mother's car keys went missing, she immediately assumed he was responsible. Upon closer review of the timeline, Amy realized that she had driven to the gym after Josh boarded the school bus, so he couldn't possibly be at fault. In spite of his innocence, however, Amy experienced genuine frustration and anger when she thought her son was to blame for the elusive car keys.

Exposure to trauma causes an automatic response: people begin to assume, anticipate, and grow anxious about the negative events they expect to occur. New adoptive parents anticipate that these feelings will be short lived, but when they persist for a long period of time, fatigue sets in and the ripple effect of the child's trauma spreads prolifically to other family members.

Straining existing relationships

Interestingly enough, the first person who has a sense of developing doom is often the person who pursued the possibility of adoption in the first place: the mother. Mothers are expected to love and protect their children, and since the traumatized child's birth mother failed at these tasks, the adoptive mom often pays a high price for her predecessor's mistakes. In addition to this dynamic, it is usually in a mother's nature to pay close attention to what her kids are doing and feeling, and she can usually predict—with startling accuracy—which shoe will drop next.

Parenting a hurt child may even intensify these innate skills. As a result of the child's trauma, it is possible for the mother to be consumed by fears that ultimately compromise her relationships with her husband and her other children. As we mentioned in Chapter 1, the hurt child often does not exhibit his worst behaviors when the father is around, so the mother is most often the one on the receiving end of the craziness. Because the dad is not privy to the negative extremes, he may not understand the level of his wife's distress. He may not even notice the child's difficulties until the mother is nearly at the end of her rope. Of course, by that time, she is probably exasperated that her partner did not notice—or, in many situations, did not believe—her tales of an out-of-control child.

This split in the parental relationship is yet another kind of transferred trauma. The mother may feel unsupported by her husband and emotionally isolated. If there are other children in the family, they are likely to experience cognitive dissonance—the feeling of discomfort that results from having two conflicting beliefs. On the one hand, the new child is part of the family, but on the other hand, he seems like such a misfit.

Why is our new brother so weird, and why would anyone act that way?

Why is he so mean to our mother, and why does our dad seem to get along with him when no one else does?

He is so embarrassing at school, and all of the kids keep asking me what's wrong with him.

Even some teachers think that my parents are not doing what they could do with him, and they ask what he's like at home.

He has no friends, and I hate for people to know that he's my brother. I always remind them that he's adopted—just so they don't think he's really related to me.

Family members may also unwittingly recycle the transferred trauma, spiraling it back to the traumatized child who then feels the negative impact. The pattern goes something like this.

1. The adopted child shows up in his new home with significant emotional baggage.

2. He imposes his trauma on others, which throws the family dynamic out of balance.

3. His new parents and siblings react with anger and rejection, which further hurts and alienates the child.

It is a clear manifestation of "what goes around comes around." The trauma that the child brought with him and shared with his new family becomes a boomerang and hits him hard—yet again.

Think of it as a self-fulfilling prophecy. What the child expects to happen actually happens because of what he does, and a cyclical system develops if the family cannot derail the child's repetition.

Helping the family find strategies for interrupting the negative cycle can be very productive for all parties involved.

One of the solutions often recommended by therapists—the right therapists—is a process called prescribing the symptom. Simply put, this means asking the child to do exactly what the parent has previously been asking him not to do. This sudden shift causes the child to interrupt his automatic thought and behavioral processes. The parent has violated what the child has come to expect, so he is disinclined to do what he typically does. Let's take a look at an example of how this might play out.

Tara is a six-year-old who has come to believe that tantrums are her best friends. They are always available when she needs them, they are wonderfully predictable, they are utterly reliable, and they protect her from being cooperative. What Tara has yet to learn is that cooperation might actually become her new best friend if only she would give it a try.

When Tara was living in her birth home, her tantrums were part of her survival mechanism, because they would sometimes distract her parents from their typically combative and blaring relationship. Her adoptive environment, however, was much quieter, calmer, and more stable. In fact, the only real noise came from Tara herself.

Once Tara's adoptive mom, Christine, discovered that these tantrums were her daughter's primary way of controlling her environment, she sought input from the therapist they had been seeing. Prescribing the symptom was one of the suggestions that Christine found most intriguing, so she opted to give it a try.

Tara almost always had a tantrum just as mother and daughter were in the process of leaving the house to go somewhere; school, the park, the supermarket, the bakery, Grandma's house—it didn't matter where they were headed. The mere act of getting ready to walk out of the door was enough to set Tara off.

Feeling that she had nothing to lose, Christine decided to put prescribing the symptom into play. One bright, sunny Saturday, she eagerly announced to Tara that they had to run some errands and would be leaving soon. She immediately followed her statement with, "I know you always like to have a tantrum before we go anywhere, so please start now so you can get it over with quickly."

Christine's rationale was elegant in its simplicity. If Tara complied and had the tantrum, Christine could thank her for doing precisely what she asked her to do. Score one for the mom! If Tara did not comply and refused to have a tantrum, Christine would be secretly delighted to finally be able to get the two of them into the car without a struggle. Another win for the mom team!

As the therapist had predicted and Christine had desperately hoped for, Tara assumed what she thought would be a controlling stance. "I don't want to have a tantrum today so I'm not going to! So there!"

"But I know how much they mean to you," Christine retorted sweetly. "Are you sure you don't want to have just a little one?"

Tara indignantly responded with, "I told you I don't want to have a tantrum, and you can't make me!"

Wow, what a concept! Christine thought. *This prescribing-the-symptom strategy really works wonders!* Thrilled that she had gotten her desired outcome—yet well aware that she didn't want to push her luck—she smiled at her daughter and said, "Okay, I guess we can go now, but if you decide later that you want to have a tantrum, just let me know."

Thanks to a knowledgeable therapist and Christine's willingness to try to break the cycle, Tara's automatic negative pattern was interrupted. Several times throughout that day's excursion, Christine asked her daughter if they should take a break so Tara could have a tantrum.

"No, Mom, I already told you! I don't want to have a tantrum today!"

The more frustrated Tara became with her mother's queries, the more compliant she actually was. Without realizing it, she was on her way to becoming an infinitely more cooperative little girl.

Christine was positively joyful to have found a way to break the pattern, and her automatic feelings of anger began to subside.

"I feel as if I've won a little peace in the process of getting my life back," she told the therapist when she reported the day's events. "I'm going to do everything I can to help ensure that the shift continues. It might not always work, but I finally feel as if I have some control over my relationship with my daughter. I'm not her victim any more, and I swear I'm never going back to feeling that way."

The emergence of optimism was welcome, and it was something that Christine had not felt for a long, long time.

Once parents start to feel more in control of their lives, they find that they have more energy to deal with their families the way they used to prior to the adoption. They can once again enjoy positive interactions with their other children, who may have felt somewhat abandoned due to the adopted child's over-packed agenda. Let's face it: numerous therapy appointments, parent–teacher conferences, social worker visits, and those oh-so-maddening tantrums take up an enormous amount of precious time.

While the overall nature and character of the family will probably never be the same after the addition of a new member, there's a strong possibility that everyone will eventually find a way to accommodate the level of trauma they currently live with. Also, over time, they will develop a better understanding of the situation and all its ramifications.

It is very important for parents to make every attempt to maintain the same kinds of relationship with their resident children that they previously had. When there is a breakdown, the children who were there before the adoption experience a level of trauma that is foreign and completely unexplainable to them.

Where have my parents gone? I hardly ever get to see or talk to them anymore.

Why don't we go out to eat as much as we did? I miss those fun dinners when we laughed all the time.

My friends hate to come to my house for sleepovers, and I'm really relieved about that. My sister says and does the dumbest things, and it makes me want to crawl away and pretend I don't even know her.

Sometimes, parents try to explain to their resident children what is going on, why it is going on, and why they should all try to understand the new child's difficulties. Although adoption is a parental decision, it is a decision that may alter the lives of all family members forever. In spite of the parents' explanations, the other children and adolescents may not be developmentally ready to have empathy and understanding for the person who has upended their lives. Parents who expect their other children to understand the adopted child's issues can be assured that the children will develop resentments and may even question the soundness of their parents' decision.

When it simply doesn't work

Marsha and Terry were missionaries from the UK who were working in Haiti, where they spent considerable time in an orphanage that was poorly run and insufficiently staffed. Many of the children had physical difficulties, developmental delays, and medical problems, and they had all suffered abandonment and repeated losses in their brief lives.

While Marsha and Terry grew to like many of the children, one little bright-eyed girl, Martinique, captured their hearts. It wasn't long before they seriously considered adding her to their family—a new sister for their biological children, Tyler and Taylor.

As they spent more and more time in the orphanage, they noticed that Martinique seemed to have a special connection to a younger boy, Jean. Since there seemed to be a sibling-like attachment between the two children, Marsha and Terry agreed to try to adopt both of them. Although Martinique was a bit bossy toward Jean, they chalked it up to the normal conflicts between brothers and sisters.

Marsha grew up in a large family, and she and her siblings often clashed about issues that later seemed completely unimportant. Terry was an only child, so he trusted Marsha's judgment that all would be well. They discussed adding a younger brother and sister to their family with Tyler and Taylor, who were very excited about having two more children to play with.

The new family of six headed to the UK to begin their expanded lives. They were warmly welcomed home by relatives and friends, who were thrilled about the addition of the two younger kids. Everything seemed to go peacefully and according to plan...for about two weeks.

"Goodness gracious! Where is this coming from?" shouted Marsha, as Martinique aggressively attacked Jean in a way she had never done before. Marsha had no idea what the little girl was saying because she was screaming in Haitian Creole, but it was eminently clear that this was more than a typical, harmless fight between a sister and brother. Martinique was in full attack mode, and Jean was cowering beneath her with his arms protectively over his head.

Marsha and Terry pulled the two children apart, soothed Jean by putting him in a warm bath, and restrained Martinique for about an hour. Confused and exhausted, neither of them could figure out what had just happened in their formerly peaceful home. *Now what do we do?*

Terry had contacts in the community who recommended a therapist known to have worked successfully with very challenging children. They arranged an initial consultation and scheduled three follow-up appointments. During the time between appointments, the situation at home continued to deteriorate. Marsha and Terry never let Martinique out of their sight, and she resentfully responded to this constant scrutiny by shrieking at them, giving them wicked looks, and frequently attempting to leave the room where she was being monitored. Her parents did not really want to confine her in this way, but they did not know what else to do to keep her from reeling out of control.

They were beginning to wonder if they could continue living with Martinique. The trauma she brought into the family was making them feel very victimized, and Tyler, Taylor, and Jean were terrified of their sister.

Plagued by feelings of inadequacy and guilt—yet wanting to keep the rest of their family safe—Marsha and Terry often talked long into the night about dissolving the adoption. After much deliberation with their adoption worker, they decided to explore the very difficult process of adoption dissolution. Fortunately, the agency had several families with approved home studies who were prepared to take in a child with extensive difficulties.

Let us pause here for a minute and point out that the presence of these other families was a true gift to Marsha and Terry. Knowing that others were willing to take on extreme behaviors such as those exhibited by Martinique went a long way toward easing their guilt. It doesn't always work this smoothly, but they were among the fortunate ones.

When the day of Martinique's departure arrived, the separation was marked by both tears and a strong sense of relief. The family recalibrated after several months, and they embraced the renewed balance they were experiencing.

Since Martinique's departure, they were kept abreast of her status in the new adoptive home, and, in fact, had several visits with her. Robert and Charlotte, the little girl's new parents, were very respectful of Marsha and Terry's decision to dissolve their adoption. They shared that Martinique was settling into their home very nicely, which made Terry and Marsha feel simultaneously happy and useless. While they were glad to hear that Martinique seemed to be adjusting well, they couldn't help but wonder why they weren't able to help her heal from her trauma.

Ultimately, Martinique began to flourish in the home of Robert and Charlotte, where it helped that she was an only child. Marsha and Terry learned to leave behind their feelings of failure, and they turned their full attention to Tyler, Taylor, and Jean. The three children had developed a very comfortable sibling connection, and peace once again reigned in their home.

So many adoption and mental health professionals define dissolution as a failure that is hugely damaging to the child whose adoption was dissolved. We contend that this is a perspective driven by ideology and not based on any data with which we are familiar. There are times when the trauma transferred by a hurt child cannot be managed by a particular family, yet it can be well handled and overcome by another family.

The new placement affords the child another chance to grow and heal, and it can often result in a successful adoption and life with a loving family. This is a win–win situation! The adopted child has a renewed opportunity to settle in, and the severely traumatized family that generated the dissolution can begin to mend.

Why, then, are so many people quick to judge and criticize the dissolving family? They sanctimoniously withdraw their support, yet they are quick to jump back in to point fingers and lay blame. They accuse the devastated family of breaking their commitment to become forever parents, and they often seem to draw personal validation from their tsk-tsking.

To these people we say, "Enough! You know only the cute little girl you've seen at soccer games and the community pool. You know nothing of what she's like behind closed doors. You know only her public face, which bears no semblance to the child who terrorized an unsuspecting family. So keep your opinions to yourselves, please. You are not helping, but you *are* looking self-righteous and more than a little bit foolish."

What we find so perplexing is that people seem to accept the dynamic of the private-vs.-public face when they think about adults: perpetrators of domestic violence, pedophiles, or sociopaths. So many people who are guilty of such crimes have reputations as upstanding members of the community, often known to their friends and co-workers as kind, friendly people. Those who sexually abuse children can be respected as the best coaches, clergymen, and youth group leaders. Ted Bundy was a charmer—with social skills to rival those of most men—yet he assaulted and murdered at least 30 young women over a four-year period. People hear about these dichotomies and openly accept them, but their understanding of the contradiction does not extend to children.

When families decide that they can no longer parent one or more of their adopted children, outsiders should acknowledge that there are many things about which they are unaware—that there are likely very legitimate reasons why this difficult decision was made. Surely, these parents did not enter into the adoption commitment thinking, *Well, if this doesn't work out, we'll just get rid of him.*

Even the most informed and prepared families are shocked when the traumatized child they adopted commits one heinous and dangerous act after another. It becomes critical, then, for those organizations and individuals preparing families for adoption and working with them afterward to have a very clear understanding of how trauma impacts the family unit, and to share the information openly and honestly. In a sense, the family is a macrosystem whose equilibrium is sometimes undone by the microsystem: the child who has been traumatized.

CHAPTER 5

Life after Placement

Prior to adopting a child, prospective parents are optimistic about a variety of factors: expanding their family, helping a hurt child reach his potential, and providing comfort and support to heal the emotional wounds the child sustained before adoption. Sadly, many families find that the hope and good intentions that propelled them into the adoption process begin to fade subsequent to the child's placement.

The son or daughter they thought would add something positive to the family instead spreads his pathologies around like wildflower seeds. They grow and flourish and ultimately take over, completely altering the energy of the family. Sometimes parents describe this situation as post-adoption depression—a state where hope has been extinguished and replaced by despair and regret.

"When we adopted Trevor," says Cecily, "we thought we'd be getting the birth son we'd always hoped for. My husband had visions of the two of them playing football in the yard, going on guys-only camping trips, and building a doghouse together. Instead, we ended up with a little boy who hates sports and anything to do with the outdoors, who has a terrifying obsession with all sorts of weapons and keeps trying to figure out ways to get into the securely locked gun cabinet, who lured our dog into the street right in the path of a car. We used to be a happy, childless couple with a loving golden retriever. Now we've been reduced to miserable parents with nothing but a sociopathic kid."

"Dana seemed to be the most adorable little girl at first," says Peter, her adoptive dad, "and we were thrilled to have a little sister for Lily, our birth daughter. But then she started biting. First it was Lily, then the kids at school and then she turned on my wife and me. Now it's completely out of control. No school will accept her, so we have no choice but home-schooling. We have no social life, because Dana can't be trusted around anyone. Our lives have been reduced to monitoring her constantly, and Lily is frightened to be around her. How do you explain to a six-year-old that the new sister we were all looking forward to is a monster?"

"I adopted Malia from foster care last year when she was three," explains Janet. "I hate to say this, but it's been the year from hell. Malia quickly developed a reputation as the terror of her preschool, and I'd regularly get notes from her teachers saying things like 'talks back,' 'defies direction,' 'disrupts class,' 'doesn't play well with others.' I was just waiting for 'runs with scissors,' because that seemed to be the only missing infraction.

"Last week was Malia's preschool graduation. As each name was called, the child stepped up on a little platform in the front of the room and was handed a diploma. I looked around the room and saw endless proud and smiling faces: the kids, their parents, the teachers. When it was Malia's turn, she ascended the platform to a burst of shouts and applause from her teachers. The first thought that went through my head was the obvious one: *Man, they must be so thrilled that she's leaving!*

"Now I have to go through this all over again when Malia starts kindergarten: the disruptive behavior, the dreaded parent–teacher conferences, the biweekly therapy sessions. I'm just not sure I can handle it anymore, especially as a single parent."

The sad stories are out there, and they grip us by the heart. Parents are spun in confusing circles, while children are threatened and terrorized by their new siblings. This isn't the way it was supposed to be!

The emotional charge of adoption sets families up for disappointment, and the more they romanticize and fantasize about building a family, the worse it can get. Parents envision opening their hearts and homes to a child in need—a child who will be eternally grateful for having been saved from a life of maltreatment. The truth is that a traumatized child rarely sees his adoptive parents as his rescuers, so forget about being perceived as a hero. In fact, it's more likely that you will be seen as the bad guy for ripping him out of familiar territory.

This is a topic we've touched on before, and we may bore you senseless by bringing it up again. But the fact remains that if you learn nothing more from reading this book than the one simple fact that your child will rarely see you as his savior, you will be a much better adoptive parent. Your expectations will be rooted in reality, and there's no better start than that.

Adoption can hurt—and hurt badly. If you manage to set aside your expectations and open yourself without prejudice to whatever comes, you are more securely on a path that will keep the suffering to a minimum.

Adoption from the child's point of view

To truly understand the adoption dynamic, it is crucial to consider the child's perspective. You begin your relationship as complete strangers, and that's not particularly comforting or encouraging. Why should he believe that you're going to give him a better life when you don't even know him?

When Kalisha decided to become a foster parent, she attended several workshops and seminars on parenting someone else's kids. One, in particular, left a lasting mark by using guided imagery to express the child's point of view. Kalisha explains that she was told to close her eyes and imagine the following scenario:

> I'm sitting in the living room of a modest home. The TV is blaring, my kids are bickering, and my spouse is snoring on the sofa after a few too many beers. The overall mood is pretty chaotic, but it's the norm for this imaginary family. My family.
>
> Just then the doorbell rings. I get up to answer it, and I'm greeted by two people who smile warmly and invitingly. "Go upstairs and pack a bag," they tell me. "We're moving you to a much nicer place."
>
> I comply with their instructions, then follow them out to their car. We all get in and drive for a few miles, eventually parking at the curb of a beautiful estate. The wide lawns are perfectly manicured, the landscaping is like something out of a magazine, and the house is bigger and more majestic than

anything I've ever seen. My escorts usher me to the front door, where a cheerful couple is waiting for me.

"We've been so looking forward to this!" they gush, as they step aside to let me in. I look all around, noting that the place is even more wonderful on the inside. Soft music is playing, two children are sitting at the dining table quietly doing their homework, and a big yellow dog comes up to sniff my hand. The entire scene is serene and pleasant.

"Welcome to your new home," says the woman. "I'm your new mom, this is your new dad, and this is your new brother and sister. We all love you very much, and all we ask is that you love us back. This is going to be great!" And the scenario ends.[5]

"Suddenly, I understood so clearly," says Kalisha. The first place I was in was kind of noisy and crazy, but it was mine—my house, my family. The second place was beautiful, but it wasn't familiar. It wasn't mine. Everyone in the house was a stranger, including the dog. How could these people possibly love me at first sight? How could I be expected to love them back? All I could think was that I felt better—more comfortable—in the first house. As hectic as it was, it was a true part of me. If this is how relocated kids feel, how can adoptive and foster parents possibly think that a cozy bed, a teddy bear, and a kiss will fix everything?"

Even when the birth home involves neglect and abuse, the child finds it familiar. Taking him away from what he has come to know adds another level of trauma. You are not the cowboy in the white hat on the majestic steed whisking him away to happy land. You are an unknown entity, and it may be a long, long time before he learns to trust that your intentions really are in his best interest.

Jessica and Bryce adopted Adelaide when she was seven years old. She and her two sisters had been sexually abused by their birth father—a fact that their birth mother chose to ignore for several years before reporting him. The three girls were placed in different homes, since social services felt that the severity of their shared trauma might stand in the way of healing if they were kept together.

Adelaide was quiet and withdrawn for the first few weeks of her placement, choosing to spend most of her time in her room and keeping her adoptive parents at an emotional distance. Jessica and

Bryce allowed her this quiet time, since they wanted her to make the transition to her new family at her own pace.

One drizzly afternoon, when Jessica drove to school to get her daughter, there was no sign of the child. After waiting until her car was the only one left in line, she parked and approached the teacher who had been monitoring the children's departures. He pleasantly informed her that Adelaide had been picked up by her father.

"She was so excited!" the teacher said, a big grin plastered on his face. "She squealed 'Daddy!' and jumped right in his car."

Jessica immediately called Bryce's office, already quite certain that her husband wasn't the "Daddy" who had fetched her daughter. Her next call was to the local police.

It was never determined how Adelaide's birth father discovered her whereabouts. Fortunately, his wife offered up the make, model, and license plate of his car, and the police issued an AMBER Alert[6]. Adelaide was found the same day and returned unhurt to the home of Jessica and Bryce—a place she had no desire to be.

"You're keeping me prisoner!" she wailed. "You're not my parents! I won't stay with you! Let me go home!"

Adelaide didn't care that she had warmth and security. She didn't care that the abuse was over. All she cared about was reuniting with the man she knew as her father.

Her willingness to return to the source of the crime is difficult to grasp, to be sure, but think about it for a minute. Have you ever put up with the incessant criticism of an old friend whose lifestyle has grown miles apart from yours merely because you have history together? Have you ever endured a less-than-satisfactory doctor, attorney, or hairstylist because you've been using her services for years and it's too much trouble to switch? Have you ever continued to participate in a fitness center, book club, or social group that failed to meet your needs because starting over feels like a huge chore?

While the justification behind an adult's inertia differs from that of an abused child, the core issue remains the same. The familiar is easy and predictable, and there's a huge comfort level in that. When we know precisely what to expect, we ultimately become okay with it by rationalizing the displeasure and discomfort away. Let's take a look at how it plays out.

That best-buddies-since-college pal who's a health-food junkie gets on your case yet again because you ordered a side of fries with your lunch. "But she got me through the toughest break-up of my life! I can't walk away from this friendship."

Your doctor insists on speaking to you in medical jargon that you can never understand. "But the parking near his office is so convenient!"

All the most recent selections of your book club have been historical fiction, and you're a big fan of juicy murder mysteries. "But I like all of the people in the group—okay, some of the people in the group—and the snacks are amazing."

Although a child lacks the intellectual sophistication to make excuses in this way, he is driven by the same faithful attachment to a known entity. Sadly, when a child expects to be hit, starved or sexually abused, that horrendous behavior becomes an integrated part of who he is.

So much of what traumatized children exhibit and do is related to what was done *to* them prior to their adoption. They have added their traumatic repertoire to their developing identities, and, as with anything that has become integral to who we are or who we perceive we are, the child uses what he knows to help him cope and manage his universe.

Alyssa, age 14, moved into her adoptive home after just a brief period of visiting with her new parents. Her foster home placement was unexpectedly terminated when her foster mom's father became seriously ill and the woman had to move out of state to care for him. Instead of placing Alyssa in yet another temporary home, the adoption agency decided to let her move in with her adoptive parents sooner than originally planned.

Alyssa had not even begun overnight visits before the move, and neither she nor her new parents, Ruthie and Simon, were prepared for such an unforeseen turn of events. In fact, due to the abruptness of the placement, Alyssa's social worker had not had time to share a lot of information with the family. And so they proceeded into the great unknown.

Alyssa arrived with her belongings in garbage bags—the all-too-common luggage for foster children on the move. Ruthie showed Alyssa to her new bedroom and helped her unpack.

The girl had relatively few possessions for a 14-year-old, but Ruthie shook off her feelings of sadness and decided it would give them a good reason to spend some mother–daughter time at the mall over the next few days. In the meantime, they went to a neighborhood drugstore to buy toiletries for Alyssa—she had absolutely none—and then set out to have a small barbecue.

In an attempt to help Alyssa feel like part of the family, Simon asked her to lend a hand in preparing the meal. To his surprise, he discovered that she had no idea what things were. When he asked her to bring him a spatula, she looked at him as if he were speaking a foreign language. When he asked her how she liked her burger, she replied simply, "Cooked." It was becoming clear that Alyssa had had limited exposure to items and experiences that would have been commonplace to most of her peers. Instead of assuming that she knew about everyday things, Simon and Ruthie started to think more carefully about how they handled conversations with their daughter.

After the meal, Alyssa went to her room to get ready for bed. When Ruthie and Simon went upstairs shortly afterward to say good night to her, they saw that she was in bed fully clothed. Although they thought this was very unusual behavior, they decided not to say anything about it. After all, this was Alyssa's first night with them, and they didn't want to do anything to make her feel uncomfortable.

The following morning, they noticed that Alyssa did not shower. When Ruthie peered into the bathroom, she saw that the toothbrush she'd bought Alyssa the day before was still in its packaging. Unsure of how to handle the issue, she and Simon agreed to let it slide. After several more days, they noticed that the patterns continued. Alyssa slept in her clothes every night, never showered, and did not practice any hygiene whatsoever. Finally, when Ruthie and Simon began to notice that Alyssa smelled a bit organic, they addressed their concerns with her. She immediately became irritated and defensive.

"It's my body, not yours! I can treat it any way I want to. If I don't want to be clean, I don't have to!"

Ruthie went straight to the phone and called the adoption agency to express her concerns. Alyssa's social worker shared that the foster parents had noticed the same issues—information that would have been shared at the time of placement if the move had not been so sudden.

Ruthie and Simon met with Alyssa's therapist, who explained the dynamics behind why Alyssa slept in her clothes and had intentionally poor hygiene. For years, the child had been sexually abused by her birth father in her bedroom at night. She came to believe that if she slept fully clothed and smelled bad, she could avoid his aggressive sexual advances. While these thoughts were somewhat irrational—there was nothing she could do to prevent her father from molesting her—she felt that she at least had some sort of control over what was happening in her life.

Armed with this new information, Ruthie and Simon had a better understanding of what motivated their daughter's strange behaviors. In spite of this clarity, however, they continued to feel the need to address the issues in a sensitive, open manner.

Deciding to approach the situation one step at a time, Ruthie first took Alyssa shopping for sleepwear that provided full coverage and approximated regular street wear. In this way, the young teen could still feel comfortable and secure while being able to shed her day clothes at bedtime. Ruthie's next step was to talk to Alyssa about hygiene, explaining that smelling bad could be off-putting to potential new friends. Since fitting in was as important to Alyssa as it is to most girls her age, her mother's advice resonated with her.

No child should have to go to bed feeling the need to protect herself from the doom that Alyssa faced for years. Like most traumatized children, she had devised a strategy that she hoped would help her. Even though it did not serve her when she was at risk, she felt compelled to continue the behavior. It took sensitivity and understanding on the part of her parents to gently ease her out of the habit. It took the passage of time to make her realize that she was finally safe in her bed at night—that these new parents would not hurt her.

Over time, the change can come. But keep in mind that when an abused child develops a protective mechanism, it becomes deeply ingrained. In Alyssa's case, her methodology was a failure from the start, so eventually leaving it behind was a bit easier. When the strategy works, however, it may be harder for the child to shake it.

Brayden came to live with Donna and Steve shortly after his third birthday. He had been raised by his drug-abusing birth mother and a series of her male and female partners, and he had experienced an abundance of both physical and verbal violence during his early years. As a result, he had perfected the ability to completely zone out and seal himself off from the hostility that surrounded him.

Donna and Steve witnessed this behavior from the very beginning, but they weren't too concerned about it. They laughingly referred to the child's emotional departures as "visiting Planet Brayden," and they lovingly teased him about it.

"What's the weather like on Planet Brayden?" Steve would ask.

"Are there good places to go swimming on your home planet?" Donna wanted to know.

Brayden would laugh at his parents' ribbing, but he continued to "leave the building" whenever he perceived any kind of stress. What started out as cute and harmless became disturbing as he grew older.

Brayden's zone outs had served him well during the first three years of his life. They enabled him to escape from the screaming, the hurled objects, and the flying fists that were everyday occurrences in his birth home, so he quickly got the message that it was an effective tactic. Unfortunately, he never got the message that it was no longer necessary now that he was living in a calm, stable home.

By the time he reached his early teens, the habit of mentally disappearing was having a negative impact on his life. His schoolwork suffered. His friendships were strained. And ceasing the visits to Planet Brayden became the number-one priority in therapy.

Brayden's condition is called dissociation—the state of having two or more distinct states of consciousness. It typically occurs in situations of extreme neglect and sexual abuse, and it is a process of emotionally separating from psychologically intolerable situations.

In Brayden's case, there was concern over the fact that he didn't seem to be outgrowing his dissociation. When he expressed interest in getting a part-time job at a fast-food restaurant, his parents were afraid that he would not be able to focus. They could only imagine him taking orders at a busy time and then zoning out.

During their next family therapy session, Brayden's wish to hold down a job and his parents' fear that he might not be able to perform were discussed at length. The teen admitted that he sometimes disappeared when he wanted to avoid certain people and situations. He acknowledged that, on the occasions when he would instinctively "flee," his mother's gentle tap on his shoulder would cause him to reconnect. Although this solution worked well at home and during therapy, it was not a viable tool for external situations, such as school and work.

"But I really want a job!" Brayden insisted. "If it's that important to me, don't you think I'd work really hard at doing it right?"

There were nods of agreement all around the room.

When Brayden's dad asked him what he thought would happen if he felt pressured on the job, the boy replied, "Well, I couldn't really visit my planet at work, because everyone would think I was weird or something."

Given Brayden's firm convictions, it was agreed that he could try working a few hours a week. He went for an interview, got the job, and began training. A few times, his supervisor noticed that he didn't seem to be paying attention, but she immediately brought him around with, "Dude, you have to listen to me!" Of course, no one at work had any idea that he had a problem with dissociation, so they were anything but delicate about pointing out his mental disappearances.

It wasn't long before Brayden began to develop a keener sense of his surroundings. He became more comfortable with his co-workers and customers, and his parents were thrilled to discover that he rarely had any dissociative episodes. His friends even began to notice that he remained present nearly all the time. His desire to do something independent was enough to put an end to his mental departures. Soon Brayden seemed just like all the other kids his age—failing to pay attention only when he wasn't interested in what was being said. It was no longer an escape—necessary or otherwise—it was just normal teenage stuff.

Brayden is now 18. Like many adoptees who have survived trauma, he is willing to talk about his childhood quirks. He wants to major in social work or psychology so he can help kids who have had difficult times in their early years. He often speaks to groups of foster parents and prospective adoptive parents about his life after abuse: what helped him and what didn't. His parents also share their stories with others who are considering adoption. And of all the resources available to parents who wish to adopt, there is nothing like the first-hand information that comes from real-life experiences.

Adoption as perceived by others

An additional challenge in the adoption arena is dealing with other adults who truly believe that you've done an amazing, admirable, generous, virtuous, noble, magnanimous, praiseworthy thing by adopting a child whose early life was less than stellar.

"You're so incredibly self-sacrificing for adopting an abused child!" they coo. "How wonderful it must feel to make such a difference in someone's life!"

"You just walked in and saved her from God knows what!"

"You should be so proud of what you've done!"

For starters, that kind of praise may make you blush. But imagine hearing those words on the same day that your six-year-old daughter flushes a hand towel down the toilet and floods the bathroom, and you scream inches from her face and banish her to her room. Or when your nine-year-old son unplugs the freezer in your garage and you don't figure it out until the smell of rotting meat hits four days later, at which point you none-too-gently smack his bottom and take away his bicycle, his computer, and all his privileges for two weeks. Not so noble now, are you?

Or perhaps you face issues of infertility or you don't have a sexual partner, and the still-wounded little voice in your head screams out in silent reply, "Oh, but you don't understand! I'm not trying to make the world a better place! I would give anything to be able to have a birth child instead of adopting!"

Folks on the outside see just that: the outside. They have no idea what sorts of backgrounds, behaviors, or issues you're dealing with, so they focus solely on what they perceive. The real downside is the fact that the more they praise you for the "big heart" and "eternal kindness" that led you to adopting, the more you feel as if you are a failure.

The best way to deal with the well-meaning—albeit maddening—accolades spouted by folks who simply don't understand is to smile sweetly, say thank you, and change the subject as quickly as possible.

"I hear your son's soccer team made it to the nationals. How wonderful for him!"

"Your daughter was absolutely adorable in the school dance recital!"

"I just love your new car!"

After all, one good gush deserves another. And let's be realistic here. Trying to explain your motives behind adoption is:

1. a waste of time, because unless you go into withering detail, the uninitiated are not going to understand

2. really no one else's business but your own.

We would be remiss if we didn't include something in this chapter about the "adoption obsessives." These are the people who are utterly fascinated by the fact that yours is not a birth family, and they will prod and pry to try to get personal information out of you and your children. In most cases, they are simply trying to satisfy their ignorant curiosity, and they take unbelievable liberties in their attempt to get answers.

"Can't you have children of your own?"

"Where did your little boy come from? Was he in [dramatic gasp] an *orphanage?*"

"Why did you adopt a Chinese baby? Is it really hard to get a white one?"

"Do you feel like she's really *yours?*"

"Does it seem weird when he calls you 'Mommy'?"

These are not legitimately interested people. These are rude people who have absolutely no right to poke their noses into your family. Therefore, you have absolutely no obligation to be polite or even remotely civilized.

Through personal experience, we have discovered two very effective ways to handle the adoption obsessives. All it takes is a willingness to be as bold as they are. It goes something like this.

- "It's none of your business."

- "It's none of your [insert expletive] business."

Being truthful with your child

We've talked about honesty on the part of adoption professionals. We've talked about how important it is for parents to be upfront about their concerns and fears. Now let's take a look at how vital it is for parents to be truthful with their children.

Letting a child know what to anticipate in different situations can greatly affect the outcome, turning it from a negative into a neutral, at the very least, or into a positive, if the adoption gods are on your side. For example, let's say a parent tells a child that the rollercoaster at the amusement park really isn't very scary. So the child climbs aboard, straps in, and gets frightened beyond measure when the ride speeds up and takes its first deep plunge. If, on the other hand, the parent says, "It's scary all right, but it's also really, really exciting," the child knows what will happen and is prepared for it. Scary is part of the fun, and it's precisely why people stand in line for an hour or more in the sun just to experience it.

Or take the example of a medical shot. Isabella took her son Luis to the emergency room when the three-year-old jumped over a culvert and landed in a tangle of barbed wire, cutting his scalp. The doctor had to give the child a shot on the top of his head to numb the area before stitching it, and Luis cringed at the sight of the needle.

"It will hurt a bit at first," said the doctor, "but when I sew up the cut, you won't feel a thing."

Luis grimaced when the needle went into his head, but because he was told to expect the pain, he was better able to cope with it. And when the medication took effect and the doctor started stitching him up, the child was, as promised, completely pain free.

Many children who suffer from anxiety have parents who constantly reassure them about every little thing. The result: more anxiety. Consider the mixed-messages behavior of a parent who drops a child off at a therapy appointment.

"Don't worry, honey, I'll be right outside in the waiting room if you need me," the mother says, thinking it will make her child feel more secure.

But why do I need to know where she is? the child thinks. *Why will I need her? Is something bad going to happen to me? Oh, no!*

Or what about the well-meaning parent who tries to comfort his child's fear by telling her that monsters aren't real? Yet there he is, on his knees, searching under the bed, and then dashing to the closet to peer inside. Meanwhile, as his daughter watches this absurd process, her first thought is, *If there's no such thing as monsters, why is my dad looking for them?*

Instead of trying to pave your child's way with promises of sweetness and light at every turn—promises you can't possibly keep—simply stick with the truth. It will never betray you, and it just might set an example for your child to follow. When you're honest with your child, you are preparing him for what he may encounter. And, of course, when kids tell their parents the truth, everything works out for the better. This philosophy seems so simple, yet many parents find it difficult to tell the whole truth and default to the "hole truth," which is riddled with omissions.

Yes, the truth can hurt, but it's worth the initial pain.

The power of honesty

It is somewhat perplexing to know that parents are forever advising their children to tell the truth, yet they fail to do so themselves. The truth is so easy to tell—all you have to do is report the facts. These facts, however negative they may be, are part of your child's life, so he has every right to hear them.

"Yes, your birth dad is in prison because he robbed a convenience store."

"Yes, your mom has been in and out of rehab for most of her adult life."

"No, your little brother can't live with us because he was adopted by another family, but we can make sure you get to visit him."

The honest facts—whether negative or positive—help clarify the child's life. "Protecting" him from the truth is just a pretty way of lying to him. Imagine if your child found out from someone outside the family that he was a child of rape? Astonishingly, people have an uncanny way of finding out about the personal lives of others—and people talk.

Grace was nearly two when her birth parents, Candace and Spencer, decided to move to Lake Tahoe and get married. Although they had been living together as a family for several years, the couple did not feel a pressing need to do anything official about their status before then. Their new friends and neighbors assumed they were already married, so they opted to simply make a quick trip to a local chapel to tie the knot.

When Grace was five, she came home on the school bus crying inconsolably. "Mommy, what's a bastard?" she asked between sobs. "All the kids in my class called me that today."

After doing an enormous amount of research, Candace discovered that the mother of one of Grace's classmates had somehow found out that the little girl was born out of wedlock. Her son overheard her refer to Grace as a bastard, so he used the word in school and the other children picked it up.

Candace and Spencer had never thought to tell their daughter that they weren't married when she was born. It didn't seem important, and since it didn't affect their love for her, they merely ignored the fact. But once Grace found out in such a cruel way, they had some serious explaining to do. What could have been a relatively simple conversation between parents and child had blossomed into a major issue—one that could have been avoided if Candace and Spencer had been open and honest from the start. It doesn't matter if you're an adoptive family or a birth family. Your children should be told the truth to keep information—any information—from escalating out of proportion.

Let's look at it this way. Each of us has a life mosaic that is compiled of pretty pieces, ugly pieces, and some missing pieces. In the case of a hurt child, the missing pieces are the prevailing ones. All too frequently, these holes and gaps are harder to understand and accept than even the nastiest experiences. If the parents can fill in the blanks for him, the child's life will be more complete. He will have a better understanding of who he is, where he's been, and perhaps even where he's going.

CHAPTER 6

It's Not the Child's Fault, but...

There is probably not a compassionate adult on the planet who would ever blame a child for problems in the family—unless, of course, you talk to an adoptive parent of a traumatized child who has wreaked havoc on an entire household. Additionally, that conversation would have to take place in utter secrecy under penalty of death, ideally while wearing a belted trench coat, dark glasses, and a fedora pulled down low over your brow. After all, how could such a cute little thing generate so much misery and chaos?

Ah, but he can.

Jared was nine when he joined the family of Brenda and Jeff and their two adopted children: Chad, 14, and Bonnie, 12. The two older children had been adopted shortly after birth, so taking in an older child posed a new and different challenge. Brenda and Jeff were aware of the abuse and neglect Jared had endured, so they made it a point to attend special workshops for parenting traumatized children. To supplement their course work, they also read extensively about what it might be like to raise such a child. They were ready—or so they thought.

Jared was nothing like Chad and Bonnie—unless you factored in behaviors such as eating and sleeping, which is where the resemblance began and ended. He wasn't even like the troubled kids Brenda and Jeff learned about in the workshops, who all seemed to have some redeeming qualities. Jared was wild, rude, and irreverent.

He was cold, nasty, and belligerent. He treated his parents and his siblings as if they were his fiercest enemies, and he never passed up an opportunity to remind them that they were not, and never would be, his "real" family.

"He's a complete jerk and he totally creeps me out," said Bonnie after the first week.

"I hate him," announced Chad after week number two.

"What the heck do we do now?" Brenda and Jeff asked each other after a month of utter disruption.

Welcome to family therapy, folks.

Their caseworker immediately referred them to a therapist who had a lot of experience with adoption, trauma, and difficult placements. Typically, the therapist preferred the families to wait until they had spent a longer period of time with their child before taking any definitive action, but an exception was made due to the fear that this particular placement was on the verge of disrupting.

Jared had already experienced three adoptive placements that didn't work out, and everyone involved with the case wanted to preserve this prospective adoption. Jeff and Brenda were very experienced adoptive parents who had weathered many storms as foster and adoptive parents. The therapist agreed to see the family, including the other children.

After reviewing the historical information provided by both the agency and the parents, the therapist scheduled an appointment. Initially, Jeff and Brenda met with her alone and shared their extreme frustration, admitting that they had no idea how they could go forward with the adoption. After just one month of living with Jared, they were fatigued and terrified of what the future might bring.

When Chad and Bonnie met with the therapist, it became clear that they were struggling. They felt angry that Jared treated their parents so badly, and they felt intruded upon because their new little brother constantly went into their bedrooms and took whatever he wanted. Even though Jared was only nine, Bonnie thought he was being sexually provocative with her—a belief that left her feeling helpless and unsettled.

Once he crept silently into her room when she was getting dressed for school, and she didn't notice until she spotted his reflection in the mirror. He also lingered around her and her friends at every opportunity, making all the girls feel uncomfortable. The family had discussed Jared's sexual abuse issues, but those conversations did little to prepare Bonnie for the actuality of living with a person who was so highly sexualized.

When the therapist met with Jared, she clearly saw what everyone else had discussed. He was angry, impulsive, and very sexual. He admitted that he did not like this new family, and he said he wanted to move—yet again. After three sessions in which all members of the family took part, Jeff and Brenda made the difficult choice to disrupt the placement. While they felt they might be able to manage Jared, they did not feel it was in their other children's best interests for him to stay. Chad and Bonnie were paying a high price for their parents' decision to have Jared join their family, and they just couldn't live with the trauma being imposed on their kids.

Jeff called the adoption worker and shared the decision that he and Brenda had made. While the worker was clearly concerned about the disruption, he understood the facts that drove their decision. Within a few days, Jared was moved to a foster home in which he had previously lived.

When situations such as this one arise, everyone involved is stressed. While there may be momentary relief when the child is removed from the home, the family still feels the need to explain about the adoption that didn't work out to those around them: family, friends, school personnel, members of their place of worship. Of course, some people understand and respect the decision, while others quietly pass judgment.

"How could anyone break their commitment to a child in need? Didn't they know it would be tough?"

"That poor little girl! She seemed so nice when she came to our door collecting funds for orphans in Ethiopia." (Funds that went right into the child's pocket and stayed there.)

Families who disrupt or dissolve an adoption are in dire need of the same level of support and respect that is given to all members of the adoption triad: birth parents, adoptive parents, and children. There are many youngsters and adolescents who have experienced disruptions/dissolutions who go on to join other families successfully, so it is not necessarily an unhappy ending.

Admitting it and then moving on

There are two opposing dynamics at play here: the core belief that an innocent child cannot possibly be responsible for a family's descent into the fifth circle of hell, and the firsthand knowledge that that's precisely what happened—or at least it feels that way. Let's first take a closer look at the word "innocent."

"Innocent" is defined as "free from moral wrong; without sin; pure." In fact, when used as a noun, it is a synonym for "young child." No wonder it is so fundamentally difficult to think of a little one as anything but completely guilt free!

The traumatized child is innocent in the sense that he is not the originator of the ever-evolving turmoil, but that doesn't mean he's not the one generating the adoptive family's problems. While he's not personally at fault for the chaos, his baggage and background are. The key is learning to delineate between blaming the child (wrong) and acknowledging that he truly is the source of the problem (right).

Holding yourself responsible and/or glossing over the child's role in the misery/despondency/lunacy you might be experiencing is denial in its purest form. Honesty—on every level—is what's going to get you through the toughest days, so you might as well start by admitting that the darling child whose life you hoped to save is turning yours upside down. But don't worry. A combination of the correct approach to parenting, carefully chosen therapy, a period of time, and a whopping big dose of patience will get things right side up again.

Lucy and Doug adopted Paige and Mea, half siblings, when the girls were six and four. Both children had been exposed to cocaine and marijuana during their mother's pregnancies, and as a result, they experienced a variety of developmental deficits. Paige, the older girl, had difficulties with attention, language, and learning skills in first grade, while her little sister was the renowned wild child of her preschool. Phone calls from both schools and weekly parent–teacher conferences quickly became a way of life.

About Paige:

- "She's bright enough, but she's falling behind the other students because she just can't focus."

- "She has a hard time making friends because the other children can't understand her very well when she speaks, and that makes her angry. And when Paige is angry, she talks with her fists."

About Mea:

- "She kicked one of the other children in the shin so hard that he had a bruise the size of a plum. This is the second time she did it to the same little boy, and his parents are pressuring us to do something about it. So, what are *you* going to do about it?"

- "During nap time this afternoon, Mea started singing at the top of her lungs and refused to stop. Do you know what it's like to deal with a classroom full of sleepy, cranky, weepy preschoolers who are being disturbed when they ought to be resting?"

The need to oversee problems at the girls' schools—in truth, problems in general—became so intense that Lucy had to leave her job as a graphic designer at an advertising agency. Her life was reduced to a series of kid-focused tasks: fetching Paige and Mea from school in the middle of the day because their disruptions were intolerable, driving them to therapy sessions, attending counseling on her own to help her cope with parenting and feelings of inadequacy, and devising ways to keep the girls' behaviors relatively under control.

"I had no idea it would be like this," she confessed to her best friend one Friday evening. The two women were enjoying a rare quiet moment and a glass of wine—courtesy of Doug, who had offered to take the girls to the movies. "I wanted so badly to help a couple of kids who needed security and direction in their lives, but I didn't think they'd end up directing *my* life. I'm eternally grateful that Doug's income can support us, because I never thought I'd have to quit my job and be a full-time mom."

Doug was as angry as Lucy was sad.

"Those damn kids are driving me crazy!" he told his brother after a family dinner that the girls did their best to sabotage. "Lucy and I used to be so happy, and now all we do is argue about everything. Paige and Mea are out of control almost all the time, and I feel like we're prisoners in our own home. We can't ever go out, because we never know when the girls are going to have an outburst. It's a living nightmare."

The disparity between Lucy's feelings and Doug's feelings distanced the couple, compounding the problem. Soon marriage counseling was added to their list of tasks, and the joyful relationship they once shared became a distant memory.

Months went by. Therapy and counseling sessions continued. Medications were tried. Tantrums were thrown. Tears were shed on a regular basis—and not just by the girls.

"I don't think I've cried myself to sleep so often since I was in high school," admits Lucy, "and that was just about uninterested boys and untimely zits. These tears were about life—mine, my husband's, and my children's—and it looked like we were all headed in a miserable, hopeless direction."

And then—*voila!*—an almost imperceptible shift began to occur. Credit good parenting, counseling, new meds, the passage of time, or a combination of all four—credit the magical fairies who might have visited Paige and Mea during the night, if you will—but a subtle change took place and kept on going. The girls became less reactionary and more agreeable. They learned to express themselves with words, not aggressive actions. Their outbursts at home and school diminished in frequency and duration.

As the girls calmed down, Lucy and Doug drew closer together. For the first time since Paige and Mea were placed with them, they felt encouraged. Lucy was able to take on some freelance design work, which helped balance out her previous all-kids/all-the-time lifestyle.

Two years have gone by since that pivotal day, and the family is barely recognizable. Laughter has replaced the angry, raised voices. Vacations are now possible, since the girls have gained a little thing called self-control. Both Paige and Mea are doing well in school, and their friends visit their home often.

Says Doug, "It was so hard not to point a finger at the girls and accuse them of tearing Lucy and me apart. While I knew they weren't at fault, I still kept blaming them. We're the ones who were left to deal with their birth mother's mistakes, and my resentment toward her carried over to Paige and Mea. I wish I had come to my senses sooner, because I unwittingly distanced myself from my daughters because of my anger. But at least we made it, and I'm enormously grateful for that."

"We've come such a long way," adds Lucy, "and it feels so good to be on the other side. Dare I say it? I think we're actually— finally—a normal family."

How to avoid blaming the child

When the entire dynamic of a household is altered as the result of adding a traumatized child to the family, parents feel confused and helpless. When placed in such a position, the common reaction is to look for the source of the problem. You can analyze the situation logically. You can look deep into your heart. You can peer into every closet and drawer and under every piece of furniture. You can review your family history, habits, and patterns, but you're not going to find it. That's because the problem is *there*. Standing in the middle of your living room with a stolen candy bar in his pocket and a crooked grin on his freckled face. It's your adopted child, and boy—does he have an agenda for you!

It seems almost automatic—when something goes wrong, everyone instinctively starts looking for someone to blame. Whose fault is it? Could it have been prevented? And what can be done to fix it?

Typically, it is fairly easy to determine who the culprit is when there's been some sort of infraction. The kid with the chocolate smears on his face is the one who swiped the freshly baked cookies. The dog with the dirty paws is the one responsible for the mud on the carpet. However, it becomes more difficult to understand behaviors and ascribe accountability when those behaviors are out of context with one's current environment. For example, taking food and hiding it for later consumption has a context—it just isn't in the adoptive family's arena. The context for food hoarding remains the neglectful birth home, even if the child has not lived there for many years.

Adoptive parents are often perplexed by the continuing maladaptive behaviors of their children. "Why does he keep stockpiling food under his bed when he's never missed a meal—or even a snack—since he moved in with us?" As a result of their confusion, they frequently assume that they are not able to meet their child's needs effectively. "We have told him, nearly daily, that he can eat whatever he wants, whenever he wants, but he still hoards food all the time. We must be doing something wrong."

The fact is that early food deprivation may lead to severe food issues that can be ongoing, are most definitely annoying, and can be downright infuriating at times. Obviously, the blame should be placed firmly on the child's birth parents, who are the ones who initiated the problem. As the perpetrators of early maltreatment, they get that distinction. But despite the feeling that they've taken up residence in your home, they are nowhere to be found. Hence, it's easy to get angry with the child for something that is absolutely not his fault.

Instead of getting irritated when he steals food, it is smarter to remember the (past) source of the problem and focus on addressing the (current) situation.

Trying to reason with the child will lead you nowhere, so you can cross that off your list immediately. It is not likely that any cognitive interchange will alter behaviors that are emotionally rooted. Food issues are primitive, and food is primary for the child's survival. Another practice that is equally ineffective is withholding food, which is certain to drive the hoarding desires higher.

A simple strategy that was presented in *Parenting the Hurt Child*[7] offers a viable solution. While frustrated parents are somewhat reluctant to give it a try, the following will, most likely, reduce a child's anxieties surrounding food.

Simply fill a plastic container with nonperishable food that the child likes—crackers, cereal, dried fruit, popcorn—and place it on his dresser. This will allay his fears about not having anything to eat, and while he may consume much of it in the first few days, his overriding obsession will eventually begin to dwindle. Don't worry too much about ants, bugs, and mice; if the container is properly sealed, you won't have a problem. It may mean sneaking into the child's room now and then to ensure that the container's lid is firmly attached, but that's a small price to pay.

By thinking outside the box, you just may allow your little guy to feel more comfortable about going to bed. He knows there's a food source right at hand, and that's important to him. Children who have not been in control of much of anything in their early years may feel more secure knowing that they are now allowed to be in charge of something—even if it's just the food in their rooms.

It is essential to remember that blaming does not correct much of anything. Instead, holding the child accountable in a nurturing manner will avoid the blame game that often becomes like a dog chasing its tail. Parents can try something like this: "We know it's not your fault that you are so concerned about food. It started in your birth family, where your parents did not give you enough to eat, but it is our job to help you learn to trust that we will always have food for you."

This same tone and approach can be used for many of the issues that are truly not the child's fault. The adoptive family and the child must work jointly on problem resolution in an effort to create a higher level of comfort among all family members.

Why placing blame makes no sense

Once a family gets into the habit of pointing fingers, there is a great risk that the behavior will become circular. Each member of the family blames another, and problem resolution becomes impossible. When psychological and behavioral dysfunction is the issue, it's obvious—although not particularly productive—where to place the blame.

Parents accuse their 13-year-old adopted daughter—who was consistently beaten by her birth parents—of being a bully in school because she is physically aggressive with her classmates. Is that really her fault?

A husband and wife fight constantly because their ten-year-old adopted son—who has never been able to control anything in his young life—feels powerful when he successfully plays them off one another and they get sucked into his manipulation. Every. Single. Time. Is that really his fault?

Now let's shift the focus from a traumatized child to one who has a chronic or terminal illness. It is common knowledge among medical and mental health professionals that families with a physically ill child experience intense stress. Their typically well-modulated family dynamics are thrown into a tailspin, and all members of the family are often negatively impacted by the child who is seriously ill. The parents are consumed by fear of a new diagnosis or even terrified that their child might die. Their lives become regulated by medical appointments, hospitalizations, surgeries, relapses, and treatment, all of which are often followed by more sickness. If there are other children in the family, they probably do not have the same quality of parenting that they knew before illness struck their sibling. They may not be able to continue their regular routines without interruptions, and they may have to fend for themselves if their parents are concentrating their energies on the sick child. To compound a bad situation, everyone has to witness the consequences that the sick child must endure.

It is highly doubtful that anyone would even come close to blaming the sick child for turning the family upside down. It would not make the remotest sense to lay responsibility on the very person whose life is being intensely impacted or potentially ended by a disease.

Yet the temptation to blame the adopted child for marital discord or family chaos is often strong. Although there is a significant difference between a serious physical illness and a serious psychological one, both negatively affect family dynamics. To blame the child in either instance is just plain wrong.

The role of the brain

The mental health profession is now beginning to recognize that more and more issues once assumed to be purely psychological are, in fact, brain-based. As we discussed previously, physiological changes that may have lifelong consequences take place in the brains of abused and neglected children. These changes often result in high levels of dysregulation, impulsivity, and aggression. Given the fact that our brains direct our behavior, the hurt child probably has less control over the choices he makes than we have typically thought. That may be precisely why imposing consequences is simply not corrective. The brain continues to operate inefficiently, producing the same misfiring over and over again and resulting in the same maladaptive behavior patterns.

Before it was recognized that schizophrenia is clearly a physiological disorder, behavioral assumptions were made. Perhaps the most foolish was the belief in "schizophrenogenic mothers"— moms who actually *caused* schizophrenia. A popular concept from the late 1940s to the early 1970s, it blamed mothers for creating trauma in their children that led to schizophrenia in late adolescence or early adulthood. Let's take a look at an example.

A child approaches his mother and gives her a hug. She tenses up, pulling away and giving him a cold, detached response. Maybe she does this because she feels the flu coming on and she doesn't want to infect him. Maybe she's still mad at him for upending the trash can all over the kitchen floor the day before. Or perhaps she's merely in a foul mood and doesn't want to be touched by anyone. In any case, the belief was that the child gets a mixed message—she loves me/she doesn't love me—and he's eternally doomed.

For years, mental health professionals thought that mothers were to blame, and they treated schizophrenia with psychotherapy. Really? In retrospect, it sounds like witchcraft. Fortunately, the profession has come a long way since then, and medication effectively reduces or eliminates the symptoms of this thought disorder.

Autism is yet another disorder that used to be blamed on parents—specifically on cold, rejecting mothers—and which is, in all probability, biologically based. Mothers have been blamed for numerous mental health conditions in their children without any sound scientific evidence. But why blame the mom—or the child?

An additional illustration of a condition where blame makes no sense is gender dysphoria. It is interesting to note here that the most recent American Psychiatric Association's *Diagnostic and Statistical Manual of Mental Disorders* (DSM-5) has changed the name of the diagnosis from gender identity disorder to gender dysphoria— which translates to a state of unease or generalized dissatisfaction with life. Dropping the word "disorder" simultaneously drops the blame. In cases of gender dysphoria, an individual strongly prefers things associated with the opposite sex. In many cases, the individual would rather *be* the opposite sex.

For example, a three-year-old boy with gender dysphoria prefers to dress up in girls' clothes, play with dolls, and do just about anything associated with the toys and pastimes that girls typically prefer. He will also adamantly reject anything boy-like. No one knows quite why this occurs, but it is likely to be biological. At the age of three, a child is incapable of conscious decision-making. Furthermore, he does not even have a clear understanding of gender-related issues. For anyone to assign blame to the child for gender dysphoria is patently ridiculous, and blaming the parents would be equally absurd. Many parents who have sought help for gender dysphoria for their children are often disappointed to learn that psychotherapy will not change the child's interests—although therapy might be helpful for the parents who are dealing with something unexpected and difficult to understand and accept.

Neurofeedback

As we have stated, the role of the brain in the field of mental health has garnered much more interest in recent years. That seems a bit strange, since the brain is precisely the organ involved in all mental disorders—yet it is probably the only organ that professionals have, until recently, merely guessed about treating. Biofeedback, which has been around for years, uses electronic monitoring of a normally automatic bodily function to train people to acquire voluntary control of that function. More recently, neurofeedback—a type of the process—has become more popular with professionals who treat traumatized children.

There is clear recognition that the brain drives much of what once was thought to be exclusively psychosocial and/or behavioral. Neurofeedback systems are numerous, and while different philosophies drive each one of them, they all attempt to increase self-regulation and reduce dysregulation. In each case, the goal is to provide an increased sense of well-being. Neurofeedback is one more tool that is useful in improving the quality of life of traumatized children and adolescents while not blaming them.

So, who's really at fault?

In discussions about blame—at least as far as this book is concerned—there are definitely guilty parties who can justifiably be accused. They are the adopted child's abusive and neglectful birth families. Not the kids themselves. Not the new parents who so frequently get blamed by the systems with which they interact— schools, churches, synagogues, juvenile courts, therapists, and children's services.

A great deal of blaming exists in the traumatized children arena, but it is rarely directed at those who are actually at fault for creating the problem. Of course, nothing is gained by holding the birth parents accountable for their atrocious behaviors, nor is it productive in any way at all. Sadly, the damage has already been done, and social service professionals seldom witness true remorse on the part of abusive parents. However, it would be less harmful to the adoptive family—and perhaps even offer a shred of emotional relief—to firmly place the blame where it belongs.

In keeping with our stance that full disclosure is always helpful, it is ultimately constructive for the child to be able to identify the people who caused his hurt. In that way, he can stop blaming everyone around him—including inanimate objects—for his difficulties. And if adoptive parents acknowledge the same source of the problem, it will be easier for them not to blame the child—or themselves.

The lifebook and why it may not help

Most states in the United States require every adopted child to have what's called a lifebook, which contains photos and information about his life prior to adoption. In so many cases, the birth family is pictured and described in such glowing terms that one can't help but question why the child was removed from their care in the first place.

"How sweet! They're all smiling at the family picnic!" (And afterward, grinning dad crept into the bedroom of his three-year-old daughter and molested her.)

"Oh, look at the mom teaching her little boy to ride a two-wheeler!" (And three days later, she chained her son to that same bike for two hours because he wet his bed.)

The lifebook is created under the premise of being respectful to the birth family—the very people who neglected, abused, and had sex with their children. It is often designed with a positive spin in an effort to avoid appearing judgmental.

As we are fond of saying: *Really?* We shouldn't judge someone who locked her child in a closet for hours a day, every day? We shouldn't judge someone who sexualized his child repeatedly with a revolving door of strangers?

To express such kind regard for birth parents must completely confuse the child.

"If my mom and dad were so happy and had so much fun all the time, why couldn't I stay with them?"

"If they were as nice as this book says they were, why did they give me up?"

Only in the child welfare system do we tend to respect the people who are responsible for victimizing others. It is not uncommon for caseworkers to take a traumatized child to jail to visit his parents—incarcerated for the very abuse they imposed on him. Have we lost our collective minds?

As Dr. Keck's 107-year-old grandmother used to say, "The world is topsy-turvy!"

CHAPTER 7

Adopting an Adolescent

Adopting an adolescent is a viable option, although parents must be keenly aware that they will probably have to make as many accommodations as the child does. One cannot simply import a young person into the family and expect him to want to become just like them.

"Oh, you enjoy playing bridge. I know I'll just love bridge, too!"

"Oh, you're vegetarian. I can't wait to trade in burgers and hot dogs for seitan and tempeh—yum!"

"Oh, you're a church-going family. It will be such a treat to attend services with you every Sunday!"

Don't get your hopes up, because maybe it will happen and maybe it won't.

Your older adopted child comes with a history, a personality, and a host of preferences and opinions—or complete lack thereof—regarding food, clothing, haircuts, music, peers, TV shows, language, and religion. It's possible that he may want to be more like you as a means of fitting in—of belonging—but don't be upset if that's not the case—at least in the beginning. Some things simply cannot be rushed.

Also, don't be fooled into thinking, "He's a teenager. He doesn't want to be around adults. I should keep a respectable distance." Instead, parent him in the way that feels appropriate to both of you and keep him close. Spend as much time together as he's comfortable with. He may never have had a real chance to be a child, so it's okay to appeal to the little boy in him. Be the magnet that draws him to you. Be likeable. Be friendly. But also set boundaries.

Boundaries make kids feel safe. Giving them complete freedom is like pushing them out of an airplane with a parachute and providing no explanation of what to expect on the way down and upon landing. Children and teens like to know what's going to happen next, especially if they've experienced early trauma and were consistently caught off guard by the unexpected behaviors of their abusers.

You are not doing a child or adolescent any favors by allowing him to freely explore his world. The world can be a very scary place, and while permitting your child to have *carte blanche* to wander cavalierly around every unknown corner may seem liberating to you, it can be terrifying to a child—particularly one who's been traumatized in the past.

Parenting your adopted teen effectively

Adoptive parents are very often frustrated by the difficulties their children present to them. They tend to rely on traditional parenting strategies, but these techniques have been developed for more typical kids. For traumatized kids who've been brought into a family later in life, the normal types of interventions are not effective.

Siblings Evan and Eden were placed with Annie and Greg when the children were 13 and 14. They had spent their first few years in a dysfunctional birth home where life revolved around drugs: who had them, how quickly could they be obtained, and what crimes needed to be committed to pay for them. Although the children were not abused *per se*, they were neglected more often than not.

At ages two and three, Evan and Eden were removed from their home when a neighbor found them playing unattended in the hallway of their apartment building. That marked the beginning of a series of foster placements that continued until their adoption.

Because they were so close in age and had seemed to develop a sort of survival bond between them, they were always kept together. While doing so worked for the children on an emotional and comfort level, it did not always work on a behavioral level. When Eden did well in a foster placement, her brother did not.

When Evan seemed to be improving, his sister would take a nosedive. One child or the other was always the reason why their foster parents gave up and asked that both of them be removed.

This went on for more than ten years, until Annie and Greg—after much deliberation—decided to try fostering the siblings in the hope of adopting them. They were unable to have children of their own, and since most of their friends already had young teenage offspring, they thought Evan and Eden would be a good fit in their social circle.

To some degree, they were right. Brother and sister settled in rather quickly and appeared to enjoy living with Annie and Greg. They spent a lot of time with their parents' extended family—all those friends with all those teenagers. They were well liked by the other kids, and for the first time in their lives, both of them were doing well at the same time.

Things took a turn for the worst when Annie discovered that her great-grandmother's pearl ring was missing from her jewelry box. When she questioned Evan and Eden, they denied any knowledge of the theft.

"That ring belonged to someone I loved very much," she explained to them. "It's been handed down for four generations, and it means the world to me. It represents family, and that's the most important thing there is. Are you sure you don't know anything about it?"

Again, they professed their innocence.

In most cases, if a mom said those words to an emotionally healthy birth or adopted child, the kid would feel a tug at the heartstrings. Children who have internalized their mothers do not want to see their moms sad or hurting, so they would probably admit their guilt—or more likely not have stolen the ring in the first place.

But Evan and Eden, on some fundamental level, did not care if Annie was upset. As neglected children who had never securely attached to anyone, they were not affected by her sadness. She was hurting. So what? She wanted answers. So what? Their emotional connection to their mom's feelings was non-existent, so pleasing her—helping her to feel better—never even entered their minds.

When such emotional pleas don't evoke a response, parents may need to shift into creative mode to get what they want. In cases where the missing object has great sentimental meaning, the goal should be to get the property back. Period. There are many ways to do this, and all of them require thoughtful approaches.

Consider offering a reward to whomever finds the missing object, and do so without blaming anyone of stealing. Accusatory statements are guaranteed to drive the offender into defensive mode, which accomplishes nothing. Simply state that you've lost something and need help finding it. When the guilty child doesn't feel that he is being suspected, he usually tracks down the missing item rather quickly.

If the reward strategy doesn't help, try a little trick called "interrupting the fun." Say something like, "I know we had planned to go to the beach this afternoon, but I'm so upset about losing my great-grandmother's ring that I just can't leave until I find it. If you'll help me look for it and we're successful, we can get on our way sooner."

Some people might feel that employing such deception ultimately rewards the stealing, but it's just the opposite. You're actually rewarding the finding. If the missing object is very valuable, a small reward is well worth the little ruse. If, on the other hand, the item is neither valuable nor important, this might be the time to ignore the situation.

Denise, adoptive mom to Kylie, was getting tired of her daughter taking money out of her purse and the kitchen drawer where she kept a small stash of cash. The teen was hoarding the money somewhere in her room, and her apparent plan was to supplement the funds that were in her bank account so she could buy an iPad.

Frustrated with playing detective, Denise went to the bank and withdrew most of the money that Kylie had deposited. (She was a co-signer on the account, so she had no problem doing this.) She took the cash home and put it in the kitchen drawer, counting on the fact that her daughter would take the money a bit at a time—which is precisely what Kylie did.

After a few weeks, Denise asked Kylie if she thought she had enough money to buy an iPad.

"Oh, I'll bet I do!" the teen replied excitedly. "I'll just go get the money I have in my room, and then we can go to the bank to get the rest!"

Denise countered with, "Oh, that won't be necessary. I already withdrew your money from the bank. The cash is in that drawer over there, so just grab it and we can go straight to the store."

The calculating mom was sure she saw her daughter's face turn a few shades paler. Kylie, unsure of what to do, walked over to the kitchen drawer and looked inside.

"It's empty," she said, her voice wobbly as she realized she had "stolen" her own money.

"Oh, no!" said Denise. "I can't imagine who could have taken it! I'm so sorry, sweetheart. I know how much you wanted that iPad."

Denise's empathy—okay, it was feigned, but Kylie didn't know that—taught her daughter a lesson. Imagine if Denise had exposed the ruse and reacted with a comment like, "Hah! Now you know what it's like to have your money stolen. Feels lousy, doesn't it?" Her daughter's guilt would have mingled with anger at being caught, and any learning opportunity would have been lost. Instead, the little game Denise played drove her point home with accuracy.

It is important not to respond to your teen's behavior—no matter how frustrating—with anger. While it may be difficult, patience is definitely a virtue. Instead of raising your voice and turning red in the face, try using natural and logical consequences to get your point across.

Morgan, age 15, was adopted by Betsy, who lives in New England. Born and raised in Southern California, Morgan was not used to the harsh winters of Vermont. Every morning in November, as he prepared to leave for school, Betsy would remind him to zip up his jacket and put on a hat and gloves. And every morning in November, Morgan refused. Betsy got angrier and angrier, and by the time December rolled around and the ever-testy Morgan appeared at breakfast in a pair of shorts, she was downright furious with her son.

"How many times do I have to tell you—it's cold here!" she bellowed. "You're going to freeze to death if you don't put some clothes on!"

And still Morgan refused to dress for the weather.

Finally, at the suggestion of Morgan's therapist who recommended that Betsy let nature take its course, she completely stopped her pleading. And sure enough—within just a few days, Morgan started wearing the ski parka, gloves, and beanie that Betsy had bought him.

"Ya know, it's really freezing in Vermont," he said casually by way of explanation.

No more anger. No more battles of will. The kid was cold, and rather than being forced into compliance, he figured it out on his own.

The same approach can be taken toward homework. Instead of fighting with your teen night after night to complete his assignments, just stay quiet. If he doesn't get his work done, there will be consequences at school. It's his problem, not yours. After all, you've already been in tenth grade, and now it's his turn.

It is equally important not to isolate a teen when he commits an infraction. In all probability, he's already feeling as if he doesn't belong anywhere, so sending him to his room reinforces that belief and may cause him to disconnect further from the family. Your parenting decisions will be far more effective if you first ask yourself: "Is what I am about to do going to create a connection or a disconnection in the relationship with my child?" If the answer is the latter, it's time to rethink.

Most of the time, you should opt for something that will enhance the chances of a bond in the relationship. Keep him close, and utilize every moment as an opportunity to join and connect. Try derailing the conflict at hand by creating a shift in focus. At precisely the right moment, you might suddenly remember that you have to run to the store to buy a loaf of bread. Ask your teen to join you, and perhaps stop for something to eat or drink on the way home. This will interrupt the tension of the moment, and it will allow some time for you to be with your adolescent in a comfortable manner. Every issue doesn't require immediate resolution; every issue needn't be discussed *ad nauseum*. Sometimes, doing something completely unrelated replaces the need to enter into a discussion that may simply resurrect the original conflict. The phrase "we need to talk" usually strikes terror in the mind of the person on the receiving end of such a message, since it's rarely the precursor to good news.

Most infractions fade in importance after the fact, so you can wait until later to implement consequences or chose not to impose them at all. In many instances, the absence of a consequence causes the teen to think about what he did wrong as he wonders, *How are they going to punish me?*

Grounding is another type of discipline that doesn't work well. If you keep your teen housebound—away from friends and social activities—for any length of time, it will definitely generate anger on his part. The original infraction is then compounded by that anger, which inevitably bounces back and forth between parent and child and creates distance. So now you have two problems on your hands instead of one.

Parents must remember that a grounded adolescent also means grounded parents. After all, someone has to stay at home to make sure Junior complies with the terms of his punishment. If the parents leave, any grounded adolescent is bound to enjoy his freedom— usually as inappropriately as possible.

So instead of insisting that he remain housebound except during school hours for an entire grading period, since he got two Ds on his report card, hire a tutor. Better yet, if he's doing poorly in subjects you excel in, work with him to help bring his grades up. It will bring you closer together and it's not even remotely punitive.

High on the list of don'ts when it comes to parenting is corporal punishment. It never works, so what's the point? Even if it doesn't cause physical harm, hitting your teen is highly abusive and always leads to resentment on the kid's part. If you became angry with a friend, would you hit her? If you didn't like something your doctor said, would you shove him across the room?

For many years, the mental health world was anti-spanking, insisting that hitting a child teaches him to be violent. However, many parents in the 1950s and 1960s regularly spanked their children, because then it was considered perfectly normal. Those people are not child abusers, and their children did not grow up to be violent individuals who go around assaulting people. In fact, parents often report that the occasional spanking is somewhat corrective for younger children.

That said, there are numerous—quite obvious—reasons why corporal punishment is not effective with children and adolescents who have been abused. They will not be deterred by a couple of carefully placed swats—in fact, those swats may be counterproductive. One father shared that when he spanked his six-year-old adopted son, the child asked, "Is that all you got?" The boy had been hurt very badly in his birth home, so by comparison, his adoptive dad's short spanking was nothing.

By the time a child reaches adolescence, corporal punishment should be completely off the table—if for no other reason than it may precipitate an aggressive response from the adolescent and create a huge, even unsafe, mess.

In truth, parents don't have control over as much as they think they do. It is not possible to change a teen's behavior through anger, isolation, grounding, or corporal punishment. When parents give up that false sense of power, they can actually begin to control the things that are important to the family.

Parents who attempt to micromanage their adolescent's every move will find that they are not very successful. What's more, they will notice that this adult-to-be will not appreciate an overabundance of input. Most adolescents prefer adults who are genuine, approachable, and compelling—as well as interested in them and who they are becoming. There's a greater chance that individuals who are adopted during adolescence will want to get close to their parents if they are spontaneous and enthusiastic.

Adolescents do not want to have a life tutorial as they move through their days. They do not need to be corrected, instructed, and reminded that they are not doing something the proper way. When parents draw the adolescent to them in fun ways, life will be better for everyone.

Adolescence is the time to take on the developmental tasks that teens must master: separation and individuation. Typically, these tasks are automatically undertaken as adolescence emerges and the teen attempts to define who he is as a separate entity from his parents. He does this by trying on different hats to see what he prefers. Should he be a skater, a brainiac, a rapper, a jock, or a stoner? Which of these hats do his parents prefer? Which ones drive them crazy?

Parents who overreact to the new roles their adolescent is exploring may, in fact, unknowingly push him into the one they like the least. For the teen, his parents' disapproval affirms the fact that he is now a separate person from them, and he will most likely be satisfied with his new persona. He feels that he is breaking away from their shadows and becoming someone who can successfully pronounce, "It's my life, and I can decide what I am going to do with it."

Individuals who join their families during adolescence will probably not have to separate and individuate until later. Since they have not yet developed a secure attachment to their new parents, they will not be driven to pull away. Instead, they may seek to stay close and explore what becoming a member of this family is like. They may find that they actually like their parents and wonder why their peers don't seem to like their own parents so much. When they go somewhere in public, they can comfortably hang out with their parents. They don't feel the need to run and take cover, lest their friends see them at the mall or the football game with Mom or Dad.

On the day that newly adopted Alexander, age 14, was due to leave for a week of basketball camp, his dad, Rod, drove him to school. As he was getting out of the car, Alexander gave his dad a hug and kiss goodbye—in the parking lot, in front of his friends. Another parent jumped out of his truck and asked Rod, "How do you get a hug and a kiss when I can't even get my son Jason to shake my hand?"

The difference in the behavior between the two teens was due to the fact that Alexander had been living with Rod for only three months, while Jason had been with his family for his entire life. He was already on his journey to create an identity separate from his parents, while Alexander was not. He had never had a dad, so every opportunity he had to connect with Rod felt new and wonderful. One of Alexander's teachers even called Rod to tell him that she had been teaching for more than 25 years and had never heard any student talk about a dad so much. Rod explained the situation, and the teacher quickly understood.

Alexander wanted to fit in at school. He joined the football team and became good friends with several of his teammates, which was a new experience for him. But even though he was forging relationships, his peers perceived him to be strange—different. The fact that he was in a foster home caused him to reach a new level of weirdness in their eyes. Although he attempted to participate in school activities, scheduling conflicts and a lack of acceptance made it virtually impossible. In time, Alexander simply gave up.

When he was placed with Rod, he was fiercely committed to being seen as normal—and Rod was committed to helping him. As a single dad, he was able to devote a great deal of attention to his new son, which Alexander sincerely enjoyed. Rod attended all of his son's school-related activities and forged relationships with other parents and kids. Finally—Alexander's life had turned a corner for the better!

Alexander was genuinely close to Rod, and he appreciated the fact that he had the opportunity to begin a new life. His friends spent a lot of time at his house, and he was proud of his new little family. He was even happier that his friends liked his dad and wanted to hang out with him.[8]

When parents are open to becoming part of their adopted adolescent's social life, they have a window through which they can see just how well he is doing. They become clearly aware of the kinds of friends he has, and they are in an excellent position to gauge how much freedom he can handle. Involved parents will have a comfort level with their adolescent's life, and when the time comes for him to drive, have sleepovers, and attend school dances, the parents will probably sleep better knowing that their child will make good choices with good people.

Conversely, if parents see that their teen is not making good choices—whether in friends or behaviors—they can immediately set boundaries that may help him avoid some of life's pitfalls. Many adolescents appreciate some limits, and sometimes they will even ask a parent to say "no."

Parents should try to get to know what their adolescent is okay with doing and what he might prefer not doing. Just because he is 16, for example, this doesn't mean he's ready to drive. If he gives any indication that he doesn't want to get behind the wheel, by all means don't rush to the DMV to grab him a driver's manual. His comfort level may be higher in six months or a year, so give him the time he needs. If he doesn't seem keen on asking a date to the school dance, trust that he may not be ready for whatever dating means to him.

Kathleen was 15 and had lived with her new family for only five months. Her parents immediately noticed that she seemed less mature than other girls her age, and even though she seemed interested in boys, there was an obvious hesitancy involved.

As the homecoming football game and dance approached, Kathleen seemed worried about something. When Trina, her mom, asked what the problem was, Kathleen confessed that a classmate had invited her to go to the festivities but she was afraid to be alone with a boy.

"I'm sorry, Mom, but I lied and said we were going away that weekend."

Trina replied, "No problem. We'll make plans to visit grandma and grandpa, and that way your excuse will be true."

Trina was well aware that Kathleen had been sexually abused by two of her uncles and was very tentative around males. This simple resolution to a touchy situation—coupled with insight and quick thinking—saved the day for Kathleen.

Imagine if Trina had said something like, "Oh, it will be okay. You're 15, and most girls your age are interested in boys. Why don't you think about it for a couple of days?" That approach would have been developmentally out of touch with where Kathleen was at that moment in time. Trina's absolute attunement to her daughter's needs and feelings was so comforting to the girl, and the situation was perfectly resolved.

The message to parents is pretty straightforward—if your teen is not interested in doing what you think is age appropriate, respect her perspective. She must know something that you don't. Check it out and discuss it openly with her.

In cases where your adolescent acts younger than his years, you might want to try something called developmental parenting. Simply put, it means getting a general idea of his level of psychological development and responding accordingly. If he's 15 and acts his age, you can skip the next couple of paragraphs. But if he's 15 and his behaviors and emotions are more like that of a ten-year-old, he's not going to have the maturity to handle things like dating and driving. Instead of forcing him into activities typical of his peer group, let him be a little kid for a while—at least at home.

Consider playing board games designed for a younger child. Play eye-contact games, which are great for bonding. Write on his back with your finger and have him guess what you're writing: "I love you. I'm so happy you're here. You're fun to be around." Engage in any activity that brings about close interaction between parent and child. Do it as often as possible until the child tires of it or outgrows it.

Too often, adults get stuck in age referencing. There are certainly developmental age markers for many things, but in the case of children and adolescents who have been traumatized, it's wise to assume that there will be psychosocial and behavioral delays. On the bright side, these delays can be used to facilitate developmental movement.

For example, if your 14-year-old likes to cuddle, allowing him to do so has a twofold effect: it satisfies his unmet needs and helps propel him into a more mature state of development. The act-your-age mentality is not helpful, since the teen *is* acting his age—his developmental age. If that happens to be younger than his chronological age, how is he supposed to understand what "acting your age" even means?

Parents must realize just where their adolescent is in terms of his psychosocial behavior and meet him there. He will naturally move forward when the maturational process occurs. This process can be supported—but not induced. And anyway—what's the big deal if a 17-year-old likes to color and watch cartoons? It's a much more positive—and easier to handle—alternative to what many 17-year-olds do, such as drinking, smoking marijuana, and being sexually active.

Patience will pay off, and there are many potential positives associated with being an "immature" adolescent. An immature adolescent usually wants to spend more time with his parents than do his age-mates, which presents a great opportunity to solidify his fragile attachment. He may also avoid some of the risk-taking behaviors that are typical of his peers, which can be a great relief to parents. By the time he reaches 18, he is better prepared to tackle more adult-like tasks without having had many of the usual difficulties of adolescence. Again, letting him take his time will help him feel okay about who he is and who he will become.

Giving an older kid a chance

Research tells us that kids who age out of foster care are overrepresented in prisons, the homeless population, and in the mental health system. At any given time, there are more than 500,000 children in foster care due to abuse and neglect in their birth families. Every year, between 20,000 and 28,000 of them age out of the system, and the estimates of what happens to them after that are staggering: 65 percent do not complete high school; about 6 percent go to college, and fewer than 2 percent complete a four-year degree. It is estimated that 65 percent of the homeless population has been in foster care, as well as 75 percent of the incarcerated. Only 18 states extend foster services through the age of 21, while the others terminate care at age 18.[9]

Those who have been adopted have a more permanent connection to a family who can provide support and guidance over a lifetime. While someone the age of 18 is legally considered an adult, many young people continue to get support from their families long after that age. Those who enroll in colleges and universities are often assisted by their parents—at least in part—throughout their student years. Some of them will continue their education and attend graduate or professional schools, with mom and dad still lending a hand. Some of those who complete their graduate/professional work may continue to receive financial help from their parents until they gain employment and are able to become completely self-sufficient.

Young adults who do not seek education beyond high school may also need family support as they explore employment opportunities. Those who do not complete high school may need even more help from their parents for a longer period of time. Some families may choose not to support their children financially, but assuming that relationships are positive, they will at least offer emotional support.

This applies to both adoptees and children by birth. Having a family—no matter how it was created—helps ensure some sort of backup plan if the grown-up kid needs help. Clearly, adoption offers young adults a much greater chance in life than merely leaving the foster system with no level of emotional and/or financial support.

CHAPTER 8

The Power of Optimism and Love

What counts in life is not the mere fact that we have lived. It is what difference we have made to the lives of others that will determine the significance of the life we lead.[10]

This quote by Nelson Mandela could easily be the theme of adoptive parents everywhere. They take on some of the most difficult challenges imaginable, make unparalleled sacrifices, and hope that they are having a positive effect on a child's life. Even though the smart ones know that love alone cannot heal trauma, they realize that love is nonetheless a major component of the process.

As you live your life with your new little one or teen, you will learn that rising above the fray generated by adoption is a process that comprises pain, anger, fear, sadness, grief, loss, faith, and acceptance. Only after enduring them all can you move forward into true optimism and love. As a parent, you need to take time to adjust to each of these emotional markers, and it may be necessary to simply carry your load a bit more lightly during the process. As an overall rule, it is wise to practice gratitude for positive things and to practice being okay with conflicting emotions. When you get accustomed to doing this, you may find that it works for everyone in the family. After all, not many people enjoy a high level of negative arousal.

Parents who view their adoptive experience as having more positives than negatives are typically those who have been able to maintain a focus on their original intent when they decided to adopt. Their optimism and love allow them to weather more effectively the ups, downs, and sidesteps of day-to-day living.

It is important to remember that the goal of all parenting is to convert unsocialized little people into the kinds of individuals who will ultimately be able to engage in effective—and increasing—self-management as they get older. The hope is that they will move into adulthood with the skills they need to become productive, contributing members of society who will be able to help their children do the same.

Intergenerational transmission of the family's belief and value systems will occur in a typical situation without much focused and concentrated effort. However, if the family is parenting children whose foundations have been eroded by trauma, the task will take more deliberate and targeted efforts. Keeping that in mind should help adoptive parents organize and conquer their parenting activities.

Holding on to an optimistic attitude will help you feel successful when your child's four-hour tantrums turn into three-hour ones. You'll feel like a rock star when they drop to two hours, and you'll be empowered beyond belief when you're ultimately dealing with nothing more than minor fussing.

Keep in mind that all childhood development is a series of forward moves, followed by regressions, followed by more forward moves that go just a bit further than the last ones. Knowing that this pattern exists may help you view your child's regression with some optimism—and perhaps with hope that things will turn around sooner than they used to.

Typically developing kids go through the same process of spurts, plateaus, and relapses. In these cases, the range of disparity between the good and bad behavior is narrower than it is for children who have had traumatizing experiences. If your adopted child is a perfect angel for three days and then acts as if he's possessed by the devil, know that this is common among abused children. While this thought may not give you relief, it should give you some consolation.

Just remember that a period of smooth sailing with your new child is most likely to be temporary. Acknowledging this will minimize your disappointment when a regression occurs. The mistake that many parents make after experiencing days or weeks without major problems is thinking that the kid has finally turned a corner and that everything will be better going forward. A corner may, in fact, have been turned, but that doesn't mean it will last.

Realistic expectations will better prepare you for what might happen next, and they will also help you maintain a balanced optimism that will allow you to demonstrate ongoing, consistent nurturing behaviors with your child.

Parents and kids talk: what helped us make it right

We have asked both parents and children to share their strategies and advice for helping to make an adoption as strong and successful as possible. Their words are delivered with straightforwardness, honesty, and, sometimes, with the most heartwarming simplicity. We hope you will enjoy and learn from their experiences.

AUTUMN AND MATT, PARENTS TO ADOPTED DAUGHTER MARIAH (NINE) AND BIOLOGICAL CHILDREN CASSIUS (SIX) AND LYDIA (THREE)

Mariah is a family relative who came into our home as a foster-to-adopt child. When we first welcomed her, the most effective parenting strategy that worked for us was keeping her days as structured and predictable as possible. In the earliest years, the mundane functioned. All of our activities—mealtimes, snacks, TV shows, playtime, and bedtime routines—were scheduled at approximately the same time every day. Our intention was to ground her in predictability and pattern. In this way, we hoped to minimize the stress and unrest she exhibited while she was learning to settle in to another new home without the comfort of anything or anyone familiar.

When something special was planned—such as a trip to the zoo, a weekly visit to the library, or perhaps a new friend coming over to play—we prepared Mariah ahead of time with frequent reminders, such as, "Remember, after breakfast today we're going to the zoo. Then, after lunch and your nap, you can watch TV or play." These simple explanations eventually worked and helped our daughter learn to trust us and start to accept the life we are sharing together. Building that trust is so essential, especially in the beginning, and it remains a cornerstone of the parenting techniques we implement with our adopted daughter. She now expects the preparation, and she thrives when we take the time to organize events with her special needs in mind.

Now that Mariah is older, we rely on the school day to provide the rigor and discipline she needs to succeed. We see the least amount of trouble in her during the typical academic year—as long as she's allowed adequate time to exercise and sleep. Again, consistency is the most effective tactic. Our weekends can be challenging if we don't have a plan, so we tend to keep things simple and repetitious.

School breaks and vacations can pose a challenge to our family if Mariah doesn't feel that she has been adequately prepared for what to expect, such as the activities we'll be involved in and who might be joining us. Summer school helps her practice and retain the information she learned over the previous academic year, and it also provides a reliable format and natural arrangement for her summer days.

Another supportive tool we've implemented is the daily visual chart, which allows Mariah to choose activities on her own. Giving her this freedom has built her confidence and independence while allaying her innate anxieties and fears about the unexpected—a by-product of her time spent in multiple foster homes and the early traumas she experienced before becoming a part of our family.

Naïvely, we were under the impression that love would be enough to erase the pain our daughter experienced essentially from the beginning of her life inside the womb of her drug-addicted mother. We never thought that the adoption would take as long as it did, given the circumstances that sent Mariah into foster care and eventually led to adoption placement. In some ways, we were lucky to be involved in a kinship adoption since we know the history and most of the whereabouts of our daughter before she came into our care.

However, Mariah's scars are deep and her anguish remains. Her early traumas have not been eradicated—despite our persistent attempts to love them out of her with predictability, structure, a safe and caring environment, and as much medical and therapeutic intervention as possible.

Our advice to new adoptive parents is to be open to the possibility that your adoptive child may need intense therapy—and it's not your fault. Your willingness to open your heart and home to a child in need of a forever family is noble and wonderful, but it may not be enough to "fix" the past.

While you're at it, find a good therapist for yourself, because you may need one, too. And a respite provider will save your sanity and refresh you and your child during the difficult times—especially when you need a break from the intensity of learning to love and care for your exceptional little one. Learn to trust your growing intuition about your adoptive child. And love will prevail, but only a fierce kind of love born of necessity and survival. Above all, don't give up—on yourself or your child.

Adds Mariah about her experiences and feelings

My adoptive parents told me, "You're a special kid and we love you," and they threw an adoption party for me!

Her advice to new adoptive parents on how to raise their kids is beautifully elegant in its simplicity

Adoption is good and the kids are really special. When your adopted child gets sad, you should say, "You know, you are special. We love you and we care about you. That is why we adopted you," and they'll feel better!

When questioned about whether she would ever adopt a child of her own one day, Mariah answered enthusiastically

Yes. Because adoption is awesome!

Mariah's siblings, Autumn and Matt's birth children, wanted to voice their opinions about adoption, too—this is what they had to say

Cassius: "What I like about my adopted sister is when we play pretend together and laugh. Adoption is a good thing. When I'm a dad, I would like to adopt a child."

Lydia: "I love when Mariah and I play together. I love when we're outside and play 'mommy and babies.' I want to adopt a boy when I grow up."

WENDY AND WARD, PARENTS TO ADOPTED SIBLINGS FAVEN (14) AND YOHANNES (11), BIOLOGICAL DAUGHTER LAURÈN (12), AND WARD'S BIRTH CHILDREN KRISTIN (25) AND FRASER (23)

In 2005, my husband and I attended a weekend seminar on international adoption. It was an eye-opening experience, and it solidified our decision to adopt a child from Ethiopia. While we waited for a referral, we created an adoption support and social group. Being with others on the same adoption path enabled us to share experiences and stories while striving to normalize adoption and mixed-race families. An unexpected benefit of this group was connecting with the local Ethiopian community, which allowed us to learn about the culture of the country and proved to be instrumental in the years to come.

In addition, I frequented the library and learned as much as I could about attachment issues, the benefits and risks of adoption, and specifics on transracial adoption. I attended seminars facilitated by local adoption agencies, and emerged feeling like somewhat of an expert.

It was from this perceived vantage point that my husband and I welcomed a two-year-old boy named Yohannes into our family in April 2006. We traveled to Addis Ababa to receive him, and that's when we discovered that he had an older sister. We met her while in Ethiopia, and within months of returning home with Yohannes, we decided to begin the process of adoption once again.

In the meantime, life with our new son began to unfold. He was an enthusiastic, active, and happy child. Although we were strangers and he did not understand a word of English, he thrived. Initially, we stayed at home with him in order to establish ourselves as his parents. During our first few months together, I was the one to look after his basic needs in an attempt to become his primary attachment figure. But while this tactic seemed to be working for Yohannes, it left me feeling exhausted and depressed. I realized I needed to take scheduled breaks and embark on a course of counseling.

Three years later, in September of 2009, Yohannes's sister joined our family. Faven was ten, and it became clear from the start that our previous stay-at-home-as-often-as-possible plan was not going to work with her. She explored her new world with great exuberance—like a curious toddler in a preteen body. Her enthusiasm was frequently dampened by frustration, because she could not communicate effectively with us. She did not understand our routines and rules, and she did not like the food we prepared. Moreover, I think she was confused that her little brother did not remember her. He was no longer the tiny, jabbering toddler she had known. Instead, he had become fluent in English and embraced all things Canadian, and he did not understand her at all.

The Ethiopian community that we had met years ago turned out to be our family's salvation. We hired two Ethiopian women to help with communication, education, cooking, and information on Ethiopian culture. The first year after Faven joined our family was fast moving and tiring. I continued with counseling and parenting seminars to gain the support I needed, and I often sought help from family and friends.

Our two adoption experiences could not be more different. In spite of my own personal struggles, Yohannes attached quickly and was a very happy little boy. To this day—after eight years—life with him is delightful, energy charged, and fluid. I have no idea if this adjustment is the result of our family's careful preparation, planning, and intention or simply because of his temperament and personality. In contrast, after parenting Faven for five years, we are often still in survival mode. We struggle to keep up with the unpredictable nature of a child who has suffered the effects of malnutrition, neglect, trauma, and loss. She has disorganized attachment, symptoms of post-traumatic stress, depression, and cognitive challenges that make school an extremely stressful experience. Parenting her is difficult.

It is hard to measure success when confronted by conflict. It is hard to garner strength when you are so frequently falling apart. With Faven, we have had to use a different form of measurement. It would not be realistic to believe that love and stability alone can mitigate emotional damage. Our circle of support has included intense engagement with a psychology and education center for our whole family. It has been a blessing and a burden as we sift through challenging issues.

Accepting offers of help has been difficult. It is easier to hunker down and hide. However, taking care of oneself is pivotal to the overall success of family. For me, this has meant scheduling regular breaks from parenting and allowing others to care for my children—even though Yohannes and Faven, as well as my biological daughter, Laurèn, protest my departure. What's more, my husband and I have found that couples' support—both receiving it and giving it to each other—is essential. The demands of raising a child with high emotional needs leaves little energy for anything else. Booking time together, seeking outside support, and simply getting away together is fundamental to creating strength.

Success does not exist without failure. Strength does not exist without weakness. Knowing your limitations is key. There is no prescribed way to behave to ensure that your family will live happily ever after. This is true when parenting any child, but it is particularly the case when parenting a child with special needs. The point is not to question whether or not everything is a success. The point is to acknowledge those rare and precious moments when you feel successful.

Wendy and Ward's daughter Laurèn was four when Yohannes joined the family in 2006 and seven when Faven arrived in 2009. Now 12, she adds her input to her mother's story

Living with adopted kids is probably a harder road than with most other children. The good thing is that your family is going to become more special. The most important thing for parents to remember is: do not expect perfection at all.

Being part of a family with adopted children has its ups and downs. My sister and brother have been through a different life, and sometimes I don't understand it. Because Faven was adopted later, she remembers stuff from her past. I think it's in the unconscious part of her mind, but when she doesn't get what she wants—even the smallest thing— she can get pretty angry pretty fast. It doesn't happen all the time— thankfully—but it's probably one of the downsides.

I would tell other kids that it's definitely a lot tougher to have adopted siblings, and it's a lot more complicated, too. My advice is to give them a little time to settle in. The first year is probably going to be the best year, so you should always be ready for whatever happens. And you should always know your siblings' stories so you can understand and be sympathetic about what they've been through. Also, therapy helps get you through the hard times. When I have fights with my sister or my brother, it just helps to go see a therapist about it, to see what I can do to help myself calm down and get things out.

I visited Ethiopia twice with my family, and I think those trips made us stronger. I could visualize what Faven and Yohannes went through when they were younger, and it gave me a new sympathy for them—a new understanding of the way they lived. It was also a nice experience to go there all together and bond and meet new people.

Yohannes, now 11, has this to share

There are a lot of kids in Africa that my parents could have adopted, but they picked me. They love me. When I grow up, I think I'd like to adopt a child because it's better for his life.

The only bad thing about being adopted is that I don't get to see my family in Africa very much. When I go back to visit, I feel excited and worried—excited because I haven't seen them in a long time, and worried that they won't treat me the same way they did before. Also, when we go to Africa, I'm afraid that it makes my [adoptive] parents sad.

If I could give advice to new adoptive parents, I would say try to be patient—as patient as you can. And when your new child is sad, go into his room and just try to cheer him up. When I'm sad and nobody comes to cheer me up, sometimes I'll just stay in my room for the rest of the day.

When asked how he feels about being adopted after living with his new family for eight years, Yohannes replied, "Well, I've kind of forgot about it."

Faven, who is now 14, adds to her brother's story

For me, one of the hard parts about being adopted is having new siblings. I feel like my sister gets treated better than me. Also, I want to be exactly the same skin color as my [adoptive] family, and that's not possible! Telling people that I am adopted is really hard. Some of them don't understand that. I miss my country and I miss my brothers and sister.

It's emotional going back to Ethiopia and seeing how I used to live—how hard it was, how poor it was. The fun part was getting to try different food, though.

I'm sure adoption is tough on the parents, too, especially when kids get mad and say things like "You're not my mom." When I went back to Africa with my family, I think it was hard for my [adoptive] parents because people were treating my brother and me so special. Maybe my mom and dad thought, "Hey, they are my kids!" And sometimes people ask my parents why they adopted, and I think it's really hard for them to answer.

New adoptive parents should remember that their kids might be sensitive. Everyone needs time to get used to each other. There are two sides. Be patient.

I still feel like I don't want to be adopted, but that's usually just when I am mad. But when I see other kids with their mom and dad and they all have the same skin color, that's when I wish I wasn't adopted.

KEN AND JOYCE, PARENTS TO ADOPTED SON ASHTON (NINE)

Ashton was a handful from the first moment he set foot in our home. A whirling dervish of energy, he is the poster boy for attention deficit hyperactivity disorder (ADHD). But as maddening as his high spirits can be, he has an endearing quality that cannot be denied. When he smiles, hearts melt. When he laughs, the room gets a little bit brighter.

It's hard to believe that he was in and out of four foster homes before he came to live with us. He was left in the hospital by his mother shortly after he was born, but in spite of the abandonment and all those moves, he seems to have an amazing resiliency. He was seven when he joined our family, and now—two years later—we're still butting heads with this strong-willed little boy.

Parenting him has been a challenge for my wife and me. As Ashton gets older, I take over more responsibility for disciplining him. He's big for his age and Joyce is petite, and since he has a tendency to throw his whole body into his emotions, I feel better if she's kept out of harm's way.

Learning what works best has been a matter of trial and error. While time-outs are effective with our friends' kids, they're counterproductive with Ashton. Separation upsets him greatly, so sending him to his room just makes matters worse. When he's behaving badly, I usually try to find a distracting activity to give him time to gain some emotional control. I'll pick up a book to read with him, invite him to flip through the pages of a sports magazine with me or make a snack for the two of us—whatever it takes to calm him down. Once he's regained some composure, we'll revisit the infraction when he's more open to hearing my side of things.

Another ineffective parenting tool is making demands. If Joyce or I insist that Ashton stop a particular behavior, we can be sure that our words will be completely ignored. Instead, I'll sometimes suggest that he keep doing whatever he's doing: "That's it, Ashton! Keep kicking the closet door! Wow, look at those great scuff marks you're making! Mom is going to love having to scrub those off!" He's old enough to understand sarcasm and he doesn't like it very much, so it's usually enough to make him stop.

I once tried to remove Ashton physically from the kitchen table when he was fussing about his dinner. Boy, was that a mistake! First he wrapped his legs around his chair so I couldn't lift him out. When I faced him, he shoved me in the chest. It took just that one time to realize that physical force on my part generates physical force on his part, so that's now out of the question.

The parenting strategy that seems to work best with our son is gently acknowledging his emotions and feelings. This is balanced by imposing firm limits and appropriate consequences. It doesn't always come naturally, but the three of us are learning as we go.

Ashton shares his perspective

My parents are nice, but sometimes they're mean. I miss my foster mom and dad, because they are nice and they didn't be mean to me. I could play video games and watch TV whenever I wanted. In my new family, I don't get to do that very much. They boss me around a lot, too—especially when I get excited. I wanted a brother, but I didn't get one like I had in my foster home.

I try to be good, but I forget the rules sometimes, and then my mom and dad get mad. I thought they might send me back to my other mom when I'm bad, but they said they would never do that. That made me sad, but I guess it's good, too, because they say this is my forever home. I wonder how long forever means.

I wonder why my first mom—the one whose tummy I was in—forgot me in the hospital. Maybe she was like me, because I lose lots of things. My mom says I would lose my head if it wasn't hooked on my body. I don't think I would.

I miss a lot of people, but now I know a lot of different people in the neighborhood, at my school, and at church. I have a lot of friends, but sometimes they don't want to play with me. Drake always says, "Calm down, Ashton, you keep throwing the ball the wrong way! You're weird, no wonder your mom gave you away." He says his mother told him that. I wish no one knew that part.

Anyway, she didn't really give me away. She just forgot about me and went home without me. My new mom and dad told me that she had some big problems to take care of and that she couldn't take care of a baby, too. They said she wanted me to get a good mommy and daddy, and they said they are glad they got me as a son. They just want me to listen better so we can be happier.

School is hard and boring, but I like recess. It's fun, but sometimes I don't get to play in the games that everybody plays because I don't know the rules. And even if I knew them once, I forget them sometimes. When I forget too many things, one kid in my class says, "I think you ate too much lead paint." I don't even know what that is.

APRIL, SINGLE PARENT TO ADOPTED SON BECKER (14)

I've been Becker's mom since he was four years old. Perhaps the most difficult part of parenting him has been dealing with his extreme intelligence and awareness. He's very conscious of the fact that his birth mother was a drug user, and he knows what kind of effect that can have on him. A couple of months ago he said to me, "I had a lousy gene pool, so there's no hope for my future. I might as well give up now."

It's heartbreaking to hear any child speak that way, but it's even more painful when you know how utterly wrong he is. While the gene pool he ridicules was by no means pristine, there was a sharp intellect somewhere in there and Becker managed to inherit every drop of it.

Unfortunately, his belief in his inevitable failure caused him to set his brilliance aside. As my mom used to say, he was hiding his light under a bushel. His grades were dreadful, his friendships were superficial, and his outlook was abominable. And then everything turned around.

As much as I hate to admit it, it wasn't because of great parenting on my part—although I've certainly been doing my level best. It wasn't because of my optimism—although my belief in him never wavered. It was—and I pause for effect here—because of the power of a crush. A crush on a teenage girl.

Becker fell for a student in his math class, and he remembers the exact moment with great clarity. He was distractedly drawing anime pictures when the principal walked into the classroom and introduced a new transfer student. Madison was tall for her age—just like Becker—with wavy, dark hair that fell halfway down her back. According to my son, it was love at first sight. Eager to impress her, he set aside his drawings and started paying attention to the teacher. Of course he knew all the answers. The ability had been there all along—it was just dimming under that bushel.

This show-off behavior continued for several weeks, and the girl did, in fact, take notice. Best of all, so did Becker's math teacher. By the time the holidays rolled around, Becker had a date for the Christmas dance and a B+ in algebra.

The two of them are now constant companions, and even though they're young, I honestly don't mind. Madison managed to bring out the best in my son, and I secretly thank her every day for changing his outlook to such a positive one. I'd thank her directly, but I'm sure she wouldn't have any idea what I was talking about. She didn't really do anything except like him back, but that was enough to bring about a major change. Her interest in him proved that he really is worthwhile, and this new perspective has carried over into every part of his life. He's a better student, a better friend, and a much happier son. Best of all, he believes in the possibility of a real future, and that's the greatest gift of all.

MARY AND KATE, PARENTS TO ADOPTED CHILDREN STEFAN (15), JORDAN (13), NATHAN (TEN), NATALIE (NINE), AND COREY (SEVEN)

Raising any children, whether birth or adopted, has varying levels of success that ebb and flow over time. In our case, success has meant building a family and remaining committed to our children. We became parents, for better or for worse. The way our children came to us certainly contributes to some of the issues they face, but once they were adopted, their struggles became ours to support.

When faced with the most traumatizing event we have endured so far, the most upsetting thing was when others took the attitude that we could somehow get out of our situation or return one of our children into the system. Adoption is just one way of creating a family, but once it's done, the commitment shouldn't be anything less than if we had given birth to them. It's seriously doubtful that anyone would have thought to ask us those kinds of questions had the problem occurred with a biological child.

Adoption is a part of our everyday language. We never talk about it in hushed tones or try to hide it. We talk openly with our children about their birth families and why those parents were not meant to raise them, and we express how glad we are that they are with us. We talk—in age-appropriate terms—about the reasons why and we try to be honest without being hurtful, since we know that our children will always have some kind of relationship with their bio-parents that we never will.

When it comes to parenting strategies, we have tried a variety. What we have learned is that many different techniques can be effective, and our best success has been finding what works for each child. We keep the same core expectations, but the way we get there needs to match the individual.

For example, Stefan is told he cannot play sports if he comes home with less than an A or a B on his report card. But that would be unrealistic for Jordan, who struggles in school. So his stipulation is that no assignments can be forgotten or missed or he will have to quit his team. It's the same core message—schoolwork comes first—but it is applied in a different way based on each child's abilities.

We also change parenting strategies now and then, especially when one of the children has caught on to a particular technique. The best way we have found to be in control is to surprise them once in a while—it keeps them on their toes!

One of the techniques that doesn't work is begging and pleading with the kids to be good. Also, as sad as it is, we have to be cautious with praise, at least with the older two. Once they know that things are going well, suddenly things don't go so well anymore. We have found that calmly acknowledging that there are no big problems going on at the moment—but still setting the bar just out of reach—keeps them more motivated than providing praise when things go well.

Therapy has been a big part of our lives, and we have tried tons of it for Stefan, our oldest. It is hard to put into words what led us to that, but ever since he was about two or three, there was something very different about how he interacts with others. It took several tries, but eventually therapy for reactive attachment disorder seemed to fit him best. There are still plenty of struggles, but at least this diagnosis has helped us understand that we are not crazy, that there is something dysfunctional about the way he relates to others. Once we found a place where his behaviors made sense, we could find ways to make our family stronger.

Attachment therapy has taught us ways to parent Stefan that we had not thought of. Parenting kids who are not bonded—who have had to learn to rely on no one but themselves—is a very different approach. For example, when he is struggling with schoolwork, we cannot ground him or lecture him about it. While that might make some kids feel bad or guilty, it simply doesn't affect him in the same way.

Also, we have to work hard to make sure that his teachers don't fall for the innocent-nice-guy-who-just-needs-a-second-chance routine, and we need to make it clear that they must set limits. Stefan can be whoever he needs to be with different people—switching personas at will to try to control a situation—but things always fall apart on the follow-through. Much of our work is getting others to hold him accountable.

Stefan has always been like a rebellious teenager—no matter what his age—and we have had to let go of the natural instinct to protect him. We have had to teach him lessons with smaller parent-induced consequences at a much earlier age than seemed natural or comfortable to us. But whatever choices in life he makes, we are his parents and our job is to give him what he needs.

If we were to give advice to new adoptive parents, it would be to talk to parents of kids who have attachment disorder. Although not all adopted children have it, it's so common among their population—yet so hard to recognize and accept. Being aware of its possibility is really important. Reading a book or talking to others cannot fully prepare you for the challenges of adoption, but it definitely helps. No one gave us any information on what might happen until we were several years into the struggle, and it would have been nice to have been forewarned.

Also, the services available after adoptions can be very difficult to access. In many cases, we had to work through bureaucratic systems and open ourselves up to feelings of judgment before we could get support. None of this is meant to scare off adoptive parents, but it has been our reality.

If you choose to adopt, prepare to be treated like a saint. Many people will see you as someone who has done such an amazing thing by adopting, and they will also view your children as abandoned puppies. Your kids will be giving you absolute hell one day and you will be at your wits' end, and someone will make a comment about what a good thing you are doing for those poor children—as if being an adoptive parent should make us see their tantrums as beautiful!

Finally, despite all the challenges, adoption is wonderful and we cannot imagine building our family any other way.

When asked what their moms did to make them feel good about being adopted, Mary and Kate's children replied

Stefan: "They care about me and they love me."

Jordan: "They treat me well—pretty much the same as kids who have birth families."

Nathan and Natalie: "They care for us."

Corey: "Everything!"

Their advice to new adoptive parents:

Jordan: "Prepare them for the future. It's no different than raising other kids. Just act like yourself. Kids should not be treated differently just because they are adopted."

Nathan and Corey: "Adoption is a good thing to do!"

LYNNE AND BOB, PARENTS TO BIRTH CHILDREN KATE (31), KARA (29), LAUREN (25), EMILY (23), AND MICHELLE (21), AND ADOPTED CHILDREN JAKE (16), NICK (12), ALI (13), AND RYAN (NINE)

As I look back on the advice and training we received as a foster/adoptive family, I am not sure what I could have been told to make me truly comprehend the severity of the issues our children were likely to have. I was very naïve to believe that a solid, structured family with a lot of love to give would be enough to overcome some of the behaviors that we have experienced. There is so much more to a child's development and personality that is not always pliable, and there is an undeniable facet of nature that I do not believe can be overcome by nurture.

We have a little girl, Ali, who came to us as a foster daughter when she was 16 months old. She was the only child in her birth family, and the home was rife with violence. She was removed by the police at a very vulnerable time, and the effect has been devastating on her personality. When she was three, we adopted her.

Every morning, I put her on the bus for preschool. As she boarded, she would look for me in the driveway, and as soon as we made eye contact, she would stick her tongue out at me. I dismissed this ritual, thinking she was trying to be funny. But several years later, our therapist asked if any of our birth daughters had ever done the same thing. Of course not! Instead of being an early sense of humor, it was Ali's form of aggression. A few months later, the bus driver happened to mention that Ali always told her how her "other mother" gave her new clothes. She would tell the driver all sorts of stories about her birth mother—except none of it was true. That is when I began to look into taking her to therapy.

I have to admit that mental health was something I didn't give much thought to. I never felt that I would take my kids to therapy, since I assumed they would grow out of the issue of the day. But with Ali, the issue of the day became the issue of the month and grew into the issue of the year.

Suffice it to say that I didn't believe in temporary insanity until Ali came into our lives. I had never met anyone who consistently told stories that weren't even remotely true—and believed them. For example, during a confrontation, I might grab her by the shoulders to get her to look me in the eye, and she would accuse me of hitting her in the face or head. I did not understand this type of brain function. I still struggle with it, but things are a little more manageable after seven years of therapy.

In addition to Ali, my husband and I have five biological daughters and three adopted sons. All four of our adopted children came to us first as foster children, which also means that their birth parents were involved in the beginning. Once it was determined that each child would not be reunited with the birth family, we chose to adopt. In all cases, the children had been with us for more than two years, and by that time we were all attached to them.

On each child's adoption day, we always go out to dinner with the entire family, including grandparents. Beyond that, we do not commemorate their adoptions—just their birthdays. To be honest, in a combined family with nine children, there is a fine line between being loving and sensitive and making sure that the bio children do not resent the attention paid to their adopted siblings. Although our birth daughters were great with the new kids when they were young, things became more complex as the adoptees grew older and began to manifest symptoms rooted in their early childhoods. It is not easy for an eight-year-old girl who is on the receiving end of her adopted sibling's aggressive tantrums to understand why the acting-out kid is getting all the attention.

I do not believe that family traditions should be different for adoptees and biological children. All children need attention, and for some to receive more almost segregates them from the family. Sometimes, I feel that biological children should have a special celebration to show the gratitude I feel for their support on this long and arduous journey.

My advice to new adoptive parents is to read up on the possible issues you might face. Just because a child is very young, it does not mean that problems won't exist down the road. Prenatal exposure to drugs and alcohol, malnutrition, abuse and neglect—all of these issues eventually take their toll. Don't be afraid or embarrassed to seek professional help—and don't wait too long to do it. At the first sign of raging tantrums or other behaviors that seem abnormal, make an appointment with a therapist.

Our family has learned so much from our fostering and subsequent adoptions. Life is not always easy, and many people have a long road until they find contentment. The ability to have compassion and understanding for all people is truly a life skill and is so very important. To see a child in need—and then help him or her to develop into a happy, successful individual—is immensely worthwhile.

When asked what she thinks about adoption, Lynne and Bob's daughter Ali, now 13, had this to say

Adoption is really hard, and I am very emotional about it. It is something that I'll have for my whole life, and I can never go back to my other life. I would if I could, but I can't. The worst thing is to think about how I will most likely not ever see my birth parents again. Sometimes, I think about how I am really living with strangers, even though I have been here a long time. I know that my mom and dad are my family, but I was not born to them. Sometimes I want to think that I was born to them, because I actually kind of look like them.

The life of an adopted kid can be very difficult—just like what I am going through right now. My parents will never understand how I feel and what I go through every day, since they were not adopted. They do not understand how I get bullied, and how someone once made fun of me because I'm adopted. He said, "Your mom gave you away and mine didn't do that." Those words really hurt.

Ali said this when asked if she would ever adopt a child when she's older

I would adopt if I could not have kids, but it would be so hard—especially because I would know what the child was going through. I think parents who are adopted can understand their kids better because they can relate to what their kids are feeling. Parents who are not adopted just don't know what it's like. I might never see my birth mother again for my whole life, and that is very sad. I don't think my [adoptive] mom really understands that. I would like to give a kid a home, but I just know how hard it would be for her when she realizes she is not with her birth parents.

Ali has a 16-year-old brother, Jake, who is also adopted

When he was about seven, Lynne asked him if he ever thought about his birth mother. She assumed he never did, since he never mentioned her or his birth father, but Jake surprised her by replying, "Yeah, Mom, I think about her every day. I wonder what school I would go to if I lived with her, I wonder what her house looks like, I wonder if she has any other kids."

Jake's birth mother was absent from his life from the time he was three years old until he was 12. He has been seeing her for the past four years, which has been a plus for him. He sees the differences and realizes how difficult his life could have been if he had stayed with her. In Jake's words:

"I get why I was adopted and I am okay with it, but it is harder than if I lived with my birth mother. I know it wasn't safe for me to stay with her at that time. It is hard being adopted, and I often get comments about my mother leaving me. Kids can be mean when there is something different about another kid.

"I would like to adopt kids when I am older. I think I could relate to them and I would understand what it is like. I have been bullied a lot about being adopted, so I would know how to tell my kid to handle it."

RITA AND PHIL, PARENTS TO FOUR ADOPTED CHILDREN: SIBLINGS JAMES (21) AND DESTINY (19) AND SIBLINGS ORION (15) AND STARLA (12)

We adopted four children: two sibling groups who were 8 and 10 and 8 and 11 when they first came to live with us. We quickly learned that many of their thought patterns and emotional reactions were set in early childhood, making them very difficult to reshape. Over time, it became obvious that they felt they were defined by their past traumas, and in many ways they relate more to who they were then than to who they are now. "That's just the way I am," is a nearly constant refrain.

They often attempt to recreate their birth homes in our home. With our first sibling group of two, one or the other was always creating an uproar. They seemed comfortable only when the emotional temperature was raised through harsh words and arguments. Dirty and cluttered surroundings were preferable to a clean and orderly house. We will never forget finding a petrified bat amidst a pile of debris in the bedroom of one of our boys! It has taken years for them to grow accustomed to taking better care of themselves and their possessions.

It has been hard to reconcile that their physical ages are not the same as their emotional ages, and we've had to learn to parent the latter. Even as they mature physically, they tend to act and react based on their emotions instead of on logical thought. When they are having an emotional response to something, they shift into survival mode and cannot process rational thoughts. Backing off and giving them time to come out of that mode before talking through the issue has helped immensely. At those times, we have learned that it is less about getting our needs met and all about focusing on what the child requires at that particular moment.

The key to forging lasting relationships with our four has been to build an emotional connection and to embrace a relentless commitment to loving them through their struggles. In many instances, this has meant using unconventional parenting methods that have proved effective for children who have experienced trauma.

Over the years, we have tried holding therapy, intensive therapy, and trauma-informed therapy for our children. All these methodologies have had their time and place in our lives to teach us how to parent more effectively and to teach the children how to manage their emotions. Some of the counselors have helped us better understand the forces at work in our children's lives and have even become sounding boards for us as we attempt to raise adopted children.

Rita and Phil's 15-year-old son Orion was asked if he had any advice for adoptive parents

Stick with your kids and get to know them better, like the back of your hand. Be sincere about it—don't just do it to get it done and check it off your list.

Destiny, age 19, also had advice

Always find ways to praise your kids. Also, never talk bad about one kid in front of another. It gives them permission to do the same, which causes more problems.

Would Destiny adopt a child?

Yes. There are so many children out there looking for a home. I was that child once. It would be my honor to take in children and provide them with a home.

LAURIE AND THOMAS, PARENTS TO ADOPTED SONS JACOB (20) AND DENNIS (19)

We met our son Jacob when he was three years old and in a Russian hospital. His back was bruised from lying on bedsprings without a mattress. Now, at age 20, he is serving in the Air National Guard and attending college.

Nine months after adopting Jacob, we met and adopted Dennis, age three, who is also Russian. At our first meeting, he continually scratched at his upper arm. After lifting his sleeve, we discovered a burned area that was scarred and disfigured. Dennis is now serving time in prison.

The boys are not biologically related, nor are their backgrounds similar. Jacob's birth mother regularly visited and rocked him, while Dennis's mother abused him and left him alone without food. Obviously, we had two very different adoption experiences with very different outcomes. It is important to share not only our successes but also our failures, since both are instructive.

In 1997, adopting from Russia was fairly new. To prepare ourselves, we attended parenting classes, joined adoption support groups, and networked with other adoptive parents. To better understand our boys, we studied their culture, food, and language. What we didn't fully grasp then was the toxic combination of early childhood trauma and prenatal exposure to alcohol.

Our adoption agency had sent us videos and photos of both boys, and we took them to our pediatrician for his review. He never even hinted that either boy could have a fetal alcohol spectrum disorder. At the time, this issue was not widely known and understood, and the doctor simply did not have the necessary training to help us.

For years, we were in discovery about Dennis. Prenatal exposure to alcohol, followed by frequent neglect, had created a problem that we did not comprehend. Normal parenting techniques did not work. Sometimes, we pushed him to respond and grow in ways that were beyond his capabilities. This left all of us confused and exasperated. If we had known then what we know now, we might have had more success.

Jacob, on the other hand, fared much better, and one of the primary reasons behind his success was the people around him. Based on his talents and needs, we identified where he would thrive. He picked good friends—mostly from his church youth group. On his own, he would not have been able to initiate and plan for these opportunities. None of this happened by accident.

A few of his struggles include impulsivity, memory issues, money management, and self-advocacy. These are factors that put him at risk of not achieving his full potential. These days, Jacob is learning to advocate for himself. He recently told me he is glad that we can talk about these problems honestly. He is learning about how his brain works, he is identifying his strengths and challenges, and he is better able to determine when to ask for help. We deal with this one day at a time.

In contrast, Dennis was given more support services than Jacob, but it wasn't enough to address his developmental delays, persistent aggression, and impulsivity. As a child, he needed constant adult supervision, strict structure to maintain orderly routines, and continual reinforcement in order to learn. All of this was necessary for his safety and for the safety of those around him.

For children like Dennis, it is important to have a committed team to help with access to support groups, mentors, residential treatment, and respite care. It is equally critical that these services are provided in a timely manner and that parents are given the help they need to be successful over time. Unfortunately, we did not have access to this higher level of support either through the county or from our private insurance.

Given my experiences, my advice to adoptive parents is this. Finding the right support group can be the first step to helping you persevere and setting you on the right course. Such groups provide the opportunity to talk with other parents who have weathered the storms that are headed your way. They can also offer valuable advice, recommend therapists, and help you become a better advocate. The main point in cultivating these relationships is to build a network around your child and around your family, and they are key in your search for knowledge, advice, and encouragement.

Suffering in silence will not get you the help you need. You must learn how to tell your story and decide how much to share. Don't be afraid to share because of pain, rejection, or stigma, but be selective about who you trust. Think of ways they may help you and your child. It is always a risk, but it is one that is worth taking.

Not everyone will understand. I like the expression: "What others think of me is none of my business." It reminds me to stay focused on what I need to do rather than worry about what's going on in someone else's head.

CHAPTER 9

The Struggles Are Worth It

In spite of all the negative possibilities surrounding the adoption of a traumatized child, one fact remains eminently clear: adoption almost always benefits the child. The process evolves over time, and since most children who have experienced trauma have developmental delays, adoptive parents must remember that catching up takes time—perhaps more time than they estimate. Dr. Keck's younger son, who was adopted at the age of 14, used to say, "My normal life didn't really begin until I was 14, so I am that far behind where I should be."

This is the reality. Healing and moving forward takes time—lots of time. Many parents do not understand that simply getting a forever family does not bring about healing. Instead, it is the behavior of the adoptive parents that creates the healing, facilitates the growth, and promotes development.

To be sure, there are ups and downs in all families. The good news is that most of the downs fade as the well-parented child becomes an adolescent and as the adolescent transforms into the young adult. The issues that parents thought were so serious when their child was eight seem almost laughable at 16 and positively meaningless at 21.

People often think that parenting should be easy. Really? Why would anyone think that raising and nurturing another person—whether by birth or adoption—would be even remotely easy? Parenting is the toughest thing you will ever do, and it also has the potential to be the most rewarding.

When you decide to take on the challenges of raising a child who has experienced inadequate or traumatic parenting, life probably isn't going to be easy. But let's be realistic here—"easy" is rarely an attainable life goal, nor should it be. Life is complicated, and the burden of parenting falls on—guess who?—the parents!

Of course, some children are easier to parent than others, but that doesn't necessarily mean it's easy to teach any kid everything he needs to know to grow up to be stable and productive. Many of the life lessons that must be imparted are not interesting to children, nor can kids even fathom that the information will ultimately be useful. So here you are—saddled with the task of teaching Junior masses of stuff he doesn't even care about.

Parenting translates to laying the groundwork for the remainder of your child's life—the foundation he will rely on and build on as he embarks on his journey into adulthood. So gear up, folks, because you'll need to tap into every ounce of courage, stamina, and resiliency you've got to do it right. Guiding your child to become a well-integrated, complex human being is the ride of a lifetime.

Sharing your attention

The struggles that many families experience when parenting a hurt child may ultimately build stronger connections once the struggle has ended or has been resolved. In fact, parents sometimes share that their relationship with the "bad boy" of the family often turns out to be closer and stronger than the relationships with the easier-to-parent kids. This is probably due to the fact that the high-maintenance child requires more one-on-one attention as he's growing up. While it helps strengthen the bond with the neediest kid, it can be tough on his siblings.

Renee, now 15, was adopted at the age of seven. She shares that her brother Tito—now 13 and adopted at ten has "ruined my life."

"I get good grades," Renee continues, "and I never get in trouble at school or anywhere. I'm a cheerleader, I play lacrosse, and I have tons of friends. Tito is mean to our parents, he steals from me all the time, and he can't hold onto a friendship to save his life. He acts so bizarre that my friends don't ever want to come to my house.

"Our mom and dad have to do so much for him, and sometimes I feel like I'm not important to them. They don't have enough time to do anything except go to my games. Don't get me wrong—I appreciate that—but I don't get to spend much one-on-one time with either of them. Since Tito can't be trusted to stay home alone, he's always around when I want to be with my mom or dad. And when he's there, he's always making noise or fussing or demanding their attention in some way, so I don't stand a chance. The three of them go to therapy every week, so that's even more time for them and less for me. I know my parents love me, but it doesn't seem fair that Tito gets so much attention when he's a pain in the butt, and I do almost everything right."

Parents must make a concerted effort to nurture all of their children as equally as possible. While the squeaky-wheel theory tends to take over, it is the parents' responsibility to maintain some sort of balance in the family so that no one is ignored. Well-meaning moms and dads often try to help the easier kids understand the issues of the difficult child, expecting them to have empathy and to be less judgmental of their sibling's problems. The likelihood of this actually happening: zero to remote.

Imagine, if you will, that you have a good friend named Elise who also has another good friend named Sybil. Sybil's life is a constant struggle as she battles with financial difficulties, an abusive boyfriend, and frequent bouts of depression. Nearly every time you try to make plans with Elise, she turns you down because Sybil is facing yet another crisis.

"She really needs me," Elise explains. "You understand, don't you?"

Sure, the logical, compassionate part of you understands, but you're still hurt. And probably more than a bit jealous, to boot. That's precisely how the better-behaved kids feel when they constantly lose their parents' attention to their acting-out brother or sister.

In most situations, the struggle is worth it. The hurt child begins to heal and change, and he may eventually catch up developmentally. In time, he may be able to reflect on his challenging life and make some amends to other family members. The fractured relationships that once existed can be repaired, and the lives of everyone may regroup around the child who once was seemingly the source of all of the family's misery.

Alain was adopted from Haiti when he was six, and he brought a lot of struggles into his new family. For most of his school years, his parents, Maggie and Todd, felt pushed beyond what they thought they could tolerate, and they were exasperated the majority of the time. Alain and his younger brother Gilberto, adopted from Brazil, were in constant conflict. Serious conflict. Their relationship was not even remotely close to typical sibling rivalry. On one occasion, Alain threw Gilberto off the roof of the garage, resulting in a broken arm. Whenever they would wrestle, Gilberto would inevitably end up getting hurt rather badly.

Todd frequently brought up the issue of exploring the dissolution of Alain's adoption, but after he and Maggie talked at length, they came to the conclusion that their commitment to parenting him remained intact. They agreed to continue their adoption journey with him, and they concurred that they would not revisit the dissolution issue again. They were his parents, and that is the way it would remain.

Alain did well in school and was quite academically astute, excelling equally in all areas. By the time he was in tenth grade, he had his sights set on becoming a physician. He was taking advanced placement courses, and his teachers claimed that he was a joy to have in class.

As time passed, he became a bit easier to deal with. While his relationship with Gilberto did not qualitatively improve, the violence seemed to vanish. Alain started to explore colleges, and he seemed to settle into his niche in life. Although there was still tension in the family, Todd and Maggie began cautiously to develop some optimism. Alain's progress continued, and he was accepted by several universities. He majored in pre-med, did well in undergraduate school, graduated from medical school, and chose to join the military, where he is continuing his medical service to many soldiers. He turned out to be extremely successful, and ultimately his relationships with Gilberto and his parents reached a comfortable level.

"I never thought we'd see the day when Alain would be doing so well," stated Maggie. "He was such a difficult child, and poor Gilberto was his hapless victim for such a long time. But things turned around—I can't even explain how—and now Alain is a confident and happy young man. Needless to say, Gilberto is relieved and is now living his life with less fear and more freedom."

Happy endings

Over the years, we have heard stories of family struggles that are followed by just-okay outcomes and others that have resulted in utterly heartwarming successes. But no matter how individual situations turned out—no matter how tough and circuitous the road became—most adoptive parents say they have no regrets. They grew to love their children, they attached to them, and they did what they could to help them. They saw their children as part of themselves. Their connections have endured, and they will for the rest of their lives.

Would it have been easier without the struggles? Most likely. Have the journeys been productive for the adoptee? Probably. Did they manage the rough times? Mostly. But decide for yourself. Following is a montage of the-struggles-were-worth-it stories that just might provide a shift in your perspective if pessimism is creeping in.

Julian, born in Colombia, was a terror in preschool, a chronic problem in elementary school, and an overall pain for those whose paths crossed his. But by the time he reached high school, he suddenly began to settle down. He is now very focused on his technology classes, and he spends hours building robots and competing in national events. All of his once-superfluous energy is directed toward his inventions and his interest in winning competitions. His extreme enthusiasm often hits a high decibel level—and his parents are seriously considering the purchase of noise-blocking headphones—but even Julian's loud new lifestyle is so much better and more productive than the antics he pulled for years. Maybe—just maybe—this young man will find his niche in life and be a happy adult. He is clearly on the right path, and for that, his parents are ecstatic and eternally grateful.

Hyacinth, a beautiful six-year-old, was adopted from foster care. Everyone who saw her fell in love with her bright smile, expressive dark eyes, and mesmerizing personality. At home, however, it was a different story. Hyacinth frequently threw lengthy tantrums, shrieking and breaking anything within reach. Although these episodes would go on for hours at a time, she would revert to the sweet, engaging little girl immediately upon stopping. Hyacinth's parents were exasperated with her horrendous behavior. They found it hard to accept that she could make such quick recoveries while they stewed on and on. She didn't even seem to understand why they remained angry.

One day at school, Hyacinth attended an assembly that featured a local dance group. She was completely enchanted by the performance—particularly the ballet—and talked incessantly to her parents about wanting to take dance lessons. They were thrilled and delighted, particularly since she had never exhibited any interest in, passion for, or curiosity about anything. They talked with friends and were referred to a dance school that had openings for new students. They enrolled her for a minimum number of classes, wary that she might not follow through.

But Hyacinth was captivated by ballet, and her instructor shared that she had natural talent. The drama that she previously demonstrated during her tantrums transferred to her dance. She looked elegant and expressive—skillful and demonstrative. Her parents signed her up for additional classes—their fingers still crossed.

After Hyacinth had been dancing for nine months, auditions for "The Nutcracker" were scheduled. She insisted on trying out for a part, which terrified her parents. When their darling little girl didn't get what she wanted, the demon in her tended to emerge. In spite of their fears, Hyacinth's instructor encouraged them to allow the child to audition.

Ultimately, Hyacinth was chosen for a major role. When she pirouetted across the stage, she glowed and became a flawless Clara. Her parents were brought to tears as she gave life to her character with grace and apparent ease. Finally, their little girl found something that she loved, and her joy was their reward.

Happy—but different—endings

Sometimes, the ending is a positive one; it's just not the one that was expected.

Tommy was placed in a foster home shortly after he was born, and at that time, he did not seem to have any apparent difficulties or issues. Alvin and Cheryl did not want to take on a child with special needs, so Tommy seemed to be a good fit for them. As a result, they were elated to adopt him when he became legally available.

After a few years, they began to notice that Tommy had some developmental delays. By the time he started preschool, it was clear that something just wasn't right. Alvin and Cheryl consulted their pediatrician, who encouraged them to be patient.

In the middle of Tommy's first-grade year, his situation worsened. Screaming, kicking, and self-abuse became regular occurrences. His pediatrician referred his parents to a physician who specialized in children who have experienced prenatal alcohol exposure. No one in social services had mentioned anything about Tommy's birth mother drinking during her pregnancy, and since he did not have the facial anomalies commonly associated with fetal alcohol syndrome (FAS), there was no initial cause for concern.

Cheryl contacted the placing agency, and a social worker did further research into the birth mother's situation. Although a few brief references to alcohol use were uncovered, they were played down. Cheryl and Alvin were shocked, angry, and disappointed at having been deceived, but they remained committed to accessing help for their son.

Tommy saw the specialist several times. He did not meet the criteria for FAS because of the absence of the usual facial characteristics, but it was determined that, in all probability, he had been exposed to alcohol. A diagnosis of alcohol-related neurodevelopmental disorder (ARND) was made based on numerous factors, including the boy's learning difficulties, emotional and behavioral dysregulation, and impulsivity. Tommy's parents approached his school principal and teacher, and plans were made to alter his academic plan.

Fast forward to high school, where Tommy enrolled in a building-maintenance vocational program. It was there that he truly began to flourish. He participated in the optional work–study component, and his employers valued his skills so much that they offered him a full-time job upon graduation. He stayed on for several years while still living at home. When he was 20, he moved into a semi-independent living situation. He felt that he was on his own at last, and his parents were thrilled that he was able to be somewhat self-supporting with only minimal assistance from them.

Tommy was not the unflawed, easy child Alvin and Cheryl had wished for. He did not grow into the highly accomplished professional they had fantasized about. But in spite of their dreams being dashed and their hopes being unrealized, they were firmly committed to their son. When he succeeded—when he was encouraged by his strides—they took enormous pride right alongside him.

Many parents who have endured intense struggles are highly satisfied when their kids eventually find their way. Most moms and dads whose expectations were lofty feel just fine when the kid they hoped would go to an Ivy League school lands a labor job, joins a union, and becomes self-supporting.

Having a preconceived notion of what your child will accomplish is risky, at best. Even if the child is yours by birth, you can't be sure of what the future holds. When the child has none of your genetic makeup, that uncertainty expands.

Human uniqueness develops over time and is influenced by a myriad of factors, including temperament, personality predisposition, genetic loading, life experiences—both negative and positive, and perception of self and of others. When parents can truly appreciate and understand their child's individuality, they can have more realistic expectations.

What parents want does not necessarily shape the child's, adolescent's, or young adult's choices and outcomes. It is necessary to establish some sort of equilibrium that will assist both parents and child in developing a fluid connection. Perhaps the best expectation and hope parents can have is for their child to be happy and successful at whatever he decides to do in life.

A few months after Elena adopted her son, Seth, she recalled a fantasy of motherhood she'd had since she was a young teen. She saw herself as the mother of an enchanting little boy, a soccer player who would be the star of every game. Although she now had her delightful son, it was already clear that Seth would never be an athlete. Awkward in the sports arena, he was a fine young scholar, preferring to read a book than kick a ball. The reality was not a win or a loss—just different.

As Seth grew into adulthood, Elena had visions of his future. Given his academic strengths, he might be a college professor. Perhaps a department chairman. He would marry and present her with perfect, brilliant grandchildren. Just the thought of it made Elena swell with pride—but Seth had different plans.

When he announced that he wanted to work with the underprivileged in third-world countries and that he had no desire to raise a family, that dim spot in Elena's heart began to pulse. With great clarity, she suddenly saw all the beautiful fantasies she'd ever harbored. With equal clarity, she saw all the fulfilling realities that had replaced them. She looked at her son and realized that his dream was no more right or wrong than her dream for him—just different.[11]

Let him be what he wants to be. If he is happy, fulfilled, and living within the law, you have done your parenting job well.

Adoption dissolution and replacement

While there is currently much controversy in the United States regarding adoption dissolution and replacement with other adoptive families, the fact remains that there are situations in which the adoptee does much better in a new family. Much of the debate centers on the practice of families attempting to "re-home" (an invented and utterly absurd word) their difficult adopted children via the internet. Words like "offensive," "unethical," "appalling," "selfish," "callous," and "cruel" don't even begin to accurately describe this trend. We can only imagine that the children who are victims of this practice feel like they are unwanted pieces of furniture, passed on to another family with whom they might make a better fit.

However, when parents choose to use an adoption agency to help them legally dissolve an adoption because of an extremely difficult, unendurable situation, that should be considered a personal family decision—not an atrocity. Many adoptees who have had multiple disruptions—the term used for the end of an adoption that has not yet been legalized—and/or dissolutions go forward to join a new family with great success.

A disruption or dissolution represents the end of what was intended to be a permanent family situation. Parents who make the very difficult decision to terminate a once optimistic placement get very little understanding or support. They experience all the emotions that go hand-in-hand with loss, and they often endure it alone. While they witnessed their child go from sweet to sociopathic, their families and friends saw just the little charmer, and they are quick to pass harsh judgment on the parents. In many cases, the social worker who placed the child also expresses obvious disdain for the hapless mom and dad, offering no follow-up support once the child leaves their home.

Parents who make the decision to terminate an adoption rarely do so without guilt. Instead, they usually feel that they are horrible people who have failed as parents. Scores of remorse-inducing questions run through their heads: *Why couldn't we help him? Did we give it our best? What will our other kids think of us? Will they fear that they, too, will be rejected for the frustrating things they do?* Many times, the adoptive parents experience more pain and loss than does the child. By the time the adoptee has to leave the home, he is ready to go because the situation on the home front has become so conflicted and uncomfortable.

One five-year-old girl learned that she was going to be leaving her adoptive family while in therapy in Dr. Keck's office. Her sobbing, overwhelmed mother—nearly out of control with emotion—shared her decision during a therapy session with her daughter. The child, completely unfazed, responded by asking, "Will my next family have a swimming pool?"

As strange as it may sound, the mother later admitted that the child's casual question made her feel more comfortable with her difficult decision. The fact that she was feeling so much pain while the little girl was already thinking about her next stop was a clear indication of just how unconnected and superficial their relationship was.

Duane, age 13, has a placement history that reads like a fictional timeline: 15 foster homes, two adoptive placements, and one legalized adoption that was ultimately dissolved. In spite of the boy's history, Roger—a single parent—wanted to explore adopting him. Duane's adoption worker felt that maybe, just maybe, this single dad with no other children would be a good fit. Most of Duane's problems in his prior placements were with the mothers, and since there wasn't one in this family, the worker felt that he just might have a chance to make it.

Duane and Roger had a few visits, and things went relatively smoothly. This in itself meant nothing, since Duane was skilled at holding things together for brief periods of time. After a few months of successful weekends together, it was agreed that a move-in date would be planned. The transition went well enough, although there were a few bumps as Duane settled in. Knowing the boy's history, Roger expected the rough patches and continued to move forward with plans for adoption. He did not ever consider disrupting the placement—even when problems at school escalated and Duane stole money from him.

Duane continued to do well—and then not so well. Each time he stumbled, Roger was there to help remedy the issue. As time went by, the two endured the ups and downs, and Roger's commitment never wavered.

Over time, their relationship grew and their attachment developed. Duane was surprised that his new dad wasn't as mean and bossy as his other adoptive parents. In his previous placements, he had masses of rules and was always in trouble. He was constantly grounded or in his room, and he felt he had little to look forward to. He hated going home from school, only to hear one mother or another complaining about everything that he didn't do, forgot to do, or needed to do.

Each time he had to leave a home, his emotions were mixed. He was afraid of what might be around the next corner, and relieved that he was getting another chance at a family of his own. Once he moved in with Roger, he felt that he finally belonged. For once, he was truly glad that he had gotten kicked out of his former placements.

Duane was excited when Roger started talking about going to court to legalize the adoption. All parties involved were highly optimistic—Roger, Duane, and the adoption worker. When the day finally came, there was much rejoicing all around.

While the occasional challenge continued, Roger remained steadfast in his commitment to maintaining a close, connected relationship, and Duane grew to appreciate everything his dad did for him and with him. Finally, after the many failed placements and the one dissolved adoption, Duane had a father who loved and respected him—a father who was with him at every juncture of their journey together.

Proclamations and platitudes about forever families and permanent placements are feel-good comments. They do not necessarily relate to parents who live with children or adolescents who wreak havoc with fire setting, animal cruelty, or attempts at sexual activity with others—both children and adults. How extended family, friends, and professionals can so easily judge the parents who decide that they cannot live with dangerous and chaotic behavior is beyond belief. Should these moms and dads subject their other children to such trauma? There are times when they justifiably decide to pull the plug in an effort to save the integrity of their families.

As with Duane, some dissolutions are akin to missions of mercy when the child is freed from an oppressive, controlling family setting. We know of many children and adolescents who are so happy to be out of their angry adoptive homes and in homes with enjoyable parents that the dissolution was actually liberating. We firmly believe that the parents should be given the understanding and compassion that they so desperately need and that the child should be given a chance to join another family who may be better able to manage the wild waters of their traumatized child. Kid after kid has done well in a second or third placement and are thankful for having another go at it.

Maintain a positive attitude

We would be naïve—not to mention misleading—if we said absolutely all of the struggles pay off. There are certainly adoptions with less-than-happy endings, just as there are birth children who turn out to be a disappointment to their parents. If you are experiencing difficult times with your adopted child or adolescent, we can't promise that all will end well. But we can emphasize the power of holding on to optimism to carry you through the difficult times.

Many parents get pulled into the negativity initiated by the child whose worldview is comprised of all things bleak and pessimistic. It is part of the transferred trauma we have discussed, and it is a common occurrence in adoptive families.

Since the child has become accustomed to his negative feelings, they are probably his default mode—as well as his emotional safety net. If he consistently sees things as negative, he can then be pleasantly surprised when a situation goes well. On the flip side, if he were to embrace happiness and optimism, he'd risk being disappointed or hurt yet again.

Before a child's placement, it is likely that his parents were optimistic, forward-looking people capable of handling both successes and disappointments with ease—probably the polar opposite of their adopted child. To better understand how the differences play out, let's try a simile here.

Parents are like rowboats, which are moved by waves. Traumatized kids are more like kayaks, which respond to ripples. When parents start to respond to ripples, they have, in a sense, joined the child's world. However, the goal of an adoptive family is for the child to join the parents' world.

Unfortunately, the parents' world is as uncomfortable and unfamiliar to the child as the child's world is to his new parents. The psychological and social differences between the parents' perceptions and realities and those of the child may be vast, although bridgeable when there is a concerted effort on the parents' part. This effort will be most effective if the parents maintain a balanced approach and response to the child's feelings, behaviors, and attitudes.

Overreacting is not productive for either the child or the parents. The child may not even notice the intensity of his mom or dad, and the parents will inevitability feel guilty—or at least seriously uncomfortable—with their exaggerated behavior.

Parents sometimes apologize to their child for what they said or did, and while this is admirable, it can be misinterpreted. The child thinks that the apology is an admission of guilt, that everything was the parents' fault, and that the parents are wrong. This is definitely not the message you want to give him.

Something similar happens when parents try to separate the actions from the individual, as in: "Honey, I really love *you*—it's just your *behavior* I don't like." For starters, the child has already justified his bad behavior by externalizing his reason for doing what he did. Second, the concept that the parent is trying to communicate is too abstract for the child to comprehend: *You love who I am, but you don't love what I do? Huh?* In truth, we are what we do. A person who commits a crime is not separate from his actions.

Struggles—a part of life

When individuals add others to their lives, it is likely that just about everything becomes more complicated. To be sure, family dynamics grow more complicated as the number of people increases. A family of three probably has fewer struggles than a family of eight. A family whose children have had well-organized lives with no trauma probably has fewer struggles than a family whose children have had a variety of developmental interruptions.

If you are looking for a life devoid of struggle and conflict, eliminate as many people from your circle as possible. Sell your kids to the highest bidder, take your pets to the animal shelter, and move to a forest where you will have no (human) neighbors. Sound inviting? Although some of you might be chuckling, there are probably a few harried parents who are saying (in a barely discernible voice), "Sounds good to me." But trust us when we say that the peaceful quietude would not be satisfying over the long haul. Struggles are inherent in life, and once they fade, new ones pop up to replace them.

And yes—they are almost always worth it.

CHAPTER 10

Adult Adoptees Reflect on Their Lives

We have given you our take on how to keep families strong after adoption, and we've shared dozens of case histories to illustrate our advice. But the following stories are perhaps the most important of all—stories from adults of all ages who were adopted as infants and children. They openly, honestly, and without reservation reveal what it feels like to be adopted, how they view the parents who gave them up, how they see their adoptive families, and how they feel about the lives they have vs. the way it might have been if they had remained in their birth homes.

If you take away anything from this book, it is our sincerest hope that it will be the information that comes directly from the hearts of those who have so generously shared their adoption journeys with you.

MELISSA, AGE 50

As a child, I hated being adopted. I didn't look or act like anyone else in my family, and I felt very different from all of them. I think all kids feel this to some extent, but in my case, it was especially true. Once I found my birth parents, I became much more reconciled. I had both adoptive and biological relatives; I had family and ancestors. I felt connected to the past—and once I became a parent, I felt connected to the future.

When my birth mother became pregnant with me, she was in her early 20s and unmarried—an American living in a foreign country.

She had little money, almost no emotional support, and few choices. I don't know what else she could have reasonably done. I know she suffered from her decision to give me up, even though it was a wise one. When we got in touch, she told me that she missed me constantly and mourned me every year on my birthday. My birth father had no idea I existed until I contacted him, so he had no say in the matter. However, I know he feels she did the right thing.

My adoptive parents were married for nearly 50 years before my mom died. They loved each other deeply and had grown up together, and they were crushed when they were told that they could not have biological children. They adopted my sister (from a different set of birth parents) and me, and then—surprise, surprise!—they had two biological children.

My relationships with my adoptive family have shifted so often over time. My mom and I were very different, but we sympathized with one another as we grew older and came to admire and appreciate one another's personalities. She was a highly organized, hardworking, logical, and orderly person—not emotive, deeply religious, and very loyal. We became especially close when I was in my 30s, and she died of cancer when I was 41. I miss her hourly.

My father and I are also quite different and do not always understand each other. I love him dearly and am glad he has remarried and is happy. Both of my parents were very supportive of my quest to find my birth mother and were/are quite fond of her. They promptly accepted her and her relatives into our extended family.

My adopted sister had a brief but unsuccessful reunion with her birth mother. I have always felt bad about that, because she deserved a great deal more than she got from her. But that was true of her entire life. She died young.

Since my two other siblings are my parents' biological children, I cannot help believing—still—that my parents love/d them more. I don't think this preference was/is altogether conscious. I am quite different from both of my siblings. We are close, but at times we have not been. I don't think our relationships have been any more or less fraught than those in other families.

The topic of how I was told about my adoption continues to be controversial. My mom and dad claimed that they told my sister and me we were adopted from the time we were quite small. Because we were bright kids, they presumed we understood. However, I, for one, forgot until I was about eight or nine. I asked my mom what it was like to be pregnant with me, and she incredulously informed me that she never had been. I remember we were at dinner and I was appalled and horrified and burst into tears. Everyone stared at me. Suddenly, a lot of odd things began to make sense.

Overall, I feel very fortunate that I was adopted. My birth mother didn't marry for a long time and didn't have any other children, and she admits that she probably would not have been a particularly good parent. My birth father had four other children, and while I am fond of him, he wasn't in any position to have raised me, either. My adoptive mom and dad gave me excellent morals and ethics and provided a good home in a good town with love and a large extended family. They valued education, friendship, loyalty, and kindness, and I value those things also.

DEVON, AGE 28

I was adopted at the age of three. In this sense, I guess I was one of the lucky ones. I know that a lot of kids are adopted in their elementary school years or later. I feel that this is often a challenge as they are moved from foster home to foster home and never really have a sense of belonging. It is much harder to connect with and trust anyone if you are constantly moved around. I know that it is still very difficult for someone if they have been through traumatic experiences early on in life. I speak about this firsthand, because I had a very difficult life prior to my adoption.

The positive thing about my negative experiences is that I have become an example for so many parents who adopt children with behavioral or emotional disorders. I have become a symbol of hope and success. If I had never gone through any of the things I was forced to endure in my foster homes and if I'd had a perfect life with no struggles, I would not be in the position to help others as I am now. If it weren't for the sexual, emotional, and physical abuse I had to bear before being adopted, my story might have been completely different.

I remember my foster mother neglecting to feed me balanced meals while her biological son was fed hot meals three times a day. I also remember her turning a blind eye to the fact that her son had plenty of toys and would never let me play with any of them. I would literally sit in the corner of the room and watch as he played and had fun while I desperately wanted the same. My foster mother would whip and beat me just for crying. If she was angry at her son, she would take it out on me. I remember her telling me that I was nothing more than a paycheck for her and that it wasn't her fault my momma didn't want me.

At this time, I was between the ages of two and three and her birth son was about seven or eight. Frequently, she would make us take baths together and would turn them into something perverted. She'd force me do things to him that should only be done by two consenting adults. When I look back, I am so thankful that she didn't let him violate me in any other way that would cause physical harm to my body.

She didn't stop there, though. She would use me for her own selfish satisfaction, as well. After my bath, she would call me into her room, where she would be waiting nude. She would tell her son to close the door and stand guard so I wouldn't run out. She made me do things to her that no toddler should even know about, let alone do. I don't want to get into specifics, but I'm pretty sure you get the picture and can imagine the things that went on.

After going through all of that, I am beyond blessed and thankful to have been adopted when I was. It gave me a fresh start and hope for my life. Believe it or not, at that early age I knew the meaning—and feeling—of hatred. I knew all about emotional and physical pain. I even knew the desire not to exist anymore. Adoption was the best thing to ever happen to me in my entire lifetime. I am not even upset or angry that my biological parents gave me up. I know that in their addiction and lifestyle, they didn't have the means or ability to raise a child. I'm quite sure that was the most responsible decision they made in their lives.

I honestly don't remember when my adoptive parents told me that I was adopted, but I knew from the very beginning. I remember knowing when it happened and when my mother told me for the first time that they would be back to get me—permanently. My mother and father told me they wanted me to live with them and somehow I just knew. The feeling I had in those moments was unlike anything I could ever explain—absolutely the best feeling ever.

It was not an easy transition to make because of the emotional damage I had sustained. I had/have an emotional disorder called reactive attachment disorder, but today it isn't as bad as it was during the early stages of my life. Due to this problem, my relationship with my parents and siblings has not always been the best, but it has definitely gotten better and continues to improve. There have been good times and bad times, but through it all there has been love and support.

I would definitely say that my life has turned out well considering all the things that happened to me. Without a doubt, things would have been a lot worse if I had stayed with my biological parents. I could have easily fallen into addiction like they did. I admit that I have had some troubles with drug use, but thankfully I never became addicted or strung out. I realized it was not for me. I have also always had good people in my life to stand in my corner. I am thankful for that, and I cherish the relationships I have now because of it. I have done everything I wanted to in my life—with the exception of a few things that I know will happen in due time. I graduated high school and college, traveled the world, and served in the Armed Forces as a Marine. I have successful relationships and friendships, and I have found love.

I have nothing to complain about as far as my life goes. I am beginning a career in criminal justice and I am writing my own book. I am happily engaged to be married and we are hoping to start our own family soon. This life was all made possible by my father, who took one look at me at an adoption party and knew I was the little boy he and my mom wanted. He tells me he saw something very special in me at first glance.

Life is not about the destination, but rather about the journey. In life, you either adapt or perish. I have chosen to adapt and overcome. To evolve. I am grateful for the love and support of my family, and I am proud of the man I have become. More important, my parents are proud of me, and that has made all the difference.

MIMI, AGE 42

My name is Mimi. I am 42 years old and I was adopted in December 1971 when I was eight weeks old. I knew from the moment I could comprehend it that I was adopted. My parents were always open about my adoption and helped me to understand the difference between my brother, who is biologically their child, and me. He is four years older than I am and he has never accepted me as his sister. Whether it's because I'm adopted, because he never wanted siblings, or because he's just not a nice person, I will never know. Sadly, my parents never encouraged or insisted that we get along and respect each other as brother and sister. We have never had a relationship and still don't to this day. It's unfortunate, but I believe it would be that way no matter the circumstances of my birth.

Being adopted was never an issue for me. I never felt different or thought differently about my parents. I never perceived them as biological or adoptive. My parents are my parents. End of story.

My parents passed away within 18 months of each other by the time I was 30. Prior to my father's death, I requested information about my birth parents from the children's home I was adopted from. I received a very limited description of them and their backgrounds. Neither of them wanted to be found or contacted in any way, and the information provided was basic and minimally informative. I believe my birth father was perhaps deceased, because he was in the hospital being treated for tuberculosis at the time of my birth.

Shortly after I received the letter from the children's home, my father passed away. I stopped all searching at that point. I'd lost my parents and I was devastated. I no longer had any interest in the people who lovingly gave me up but were not a part of who I was and the woman I've become. I wanted my parents back—not the strangers who'd given me life, but the people who'd given me a life.

My story is short and simple. I was adopted at a time when adoptions were closed and final. I strongly support adoption and the pursuit of making families in whatever way one chooses. There are so many more options now, and I think it is a blessing for all those involved. I'm not sure if my life would have been better, worse, or even different if I hadn't been adopted. Being given up as a baby and given a family at eight weeks was my path and my destiny. It created me, no matter where I originally came from.

BRIAN, AGE 43 (DR. KECK'S SON)

My life before I was adopted was not good. I was in numerous foster homes and group homes. I had no direction. I had no purpose. I felt like I had a lot of potential, but nobody would take a chance on me. When things got tough, they took the easy way out and just passed me along to the next family.

When I was 16, I thought I would just go through life without having a family. Then I met my father-to-be, and he was a dad who never gave up. He was there for me through thick and thin, through good times and bad times.

Soon thereafter he adopted me. It's been 26 years since then, and because of him, I can say I have a family—something I never thought I